Walks \

C000192922

DARK PEAK

Terry Marsh

^AQUESTA Guide

© Terry Marsh, 2001
ISBN 1 898808 03 1

ADVICE TO READERS

Readers are advised that while the author had made
every effort to ensure the accuracy of this
guidebook, changes can occur which may affect the
contents. The Publishers would welcome notes of any
changes you find.

Maps:

The maps accompanying the walks in this book are
purely diagrammatic, and have been based on out-
of-copyright maps. They are no substitute for
Ordnance Survey Outdoor Leisure Map No. 1, which
covers all the walks and is strongly recommended.

Published by
Questa Publishing, 27 Camwood, Bamber Bridge, Preston,
Lancashire PR5 8LA
and printed by
Carnmor Print, 95/97 London Road, Preston,
Lancashire PR1 4BA

Contents

1

Saddleworth Edges

Where the bleak plateau of Black Hill drops to the valleys around Mossley, Greenfield and Uppermill, lies a most endearing walk, known locally as the Saddleworth Edges. Although quite long for children, it is mostly easy walking, but there is one steep section, and a stream crossing that can be awkward for very small children.
Not advised in poor visibility.

Total distance: 8 miles
Height gain: 835 feet
Start: Binn Green car park,
along the A635 Holmfirth-Greenfield road.
GR018044.

1   From the car park, go down steps into a small plantation, and through a stile at the bottom onto a surfaced lane. Turn left, and walk down to the dam of Yeoman Hey Reservoir.

2   Follow the obvious service track around the left (west) side of the reservoir, and keep on to Greenfield Reservoir. Turn left into the recesses of Greenfield Brook.

3   A little way further on, Greenfield Brook divides into Holme Clough (left) and Birchin Clough (right). Close by, a dark tunnel captures the waters of Birchin Clough and sends them to Dove Stone Reservoir. This is dangerous: do not be tempted to explore!

4   Go round the top of the tunnel and into Birchin Clough, following its course and crossing the brook quite low down, until you reach a narrow section near small cascades. Re-cross the stream here, just below a cascade, by jumping from one slabby platform to another. But do take care. *If you have any concern that a child can cross it safely, please turn back*.

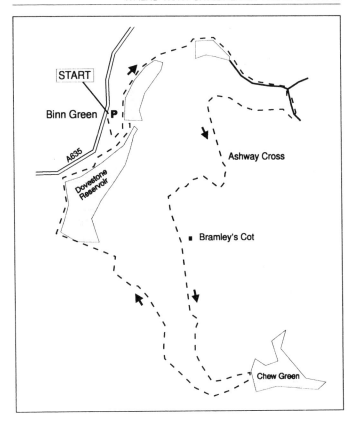

5   Beyond, the path follows the course of the brook, but you can leave it anytime to strike up the hillside on your right to a path doubling back along the line of Birchin Clough.

6   As you follow the edge path, you reach the Trinnacle, a freestanding pillar of rock, split, as its name suggests, into three, which marks the beginning of the edge walk proper. Do not allow children to clamber onto The Trinnacle.

7   From The Trinnacle, a good path wanders onwards to Ashway Cross, a memorial to a Member of Parliament killed in a shooting accident.

8   From the Cross, the path cuts inland to cross Dovestone Clough, before continuing along the edge above an escarpment.

9   Further on, a cairn and memorial is encountered, this time to two climbers killed in the Dolomites. A short way on stands Bramley's Cot, constructed against a face of rock in an ingenious way.

10 Keep on along the marginal path, with a few unavoidable patches of peat to contend with, to Chew Reservoir, one of two in England that claim to be the highest – the other is Cow Green in Teesdale.

11 Follow the reservoir service road down to the valley. Cross the Dovestones dam and on the other side either turn right onto a broad path beside the reservoir, or ascend to a stile and path above the circular overflow. The former will take you back to join your outward route near Yeoman Hey Reservoir, the latter will take you up through light woodland to meet the first lane encountered near the start of the walk, from where you climb back through the plantation to the car park above.

The Dark Peak

Also known as the High Peak, the Dark Peak, comprises much of the northern half of the Peak District National Park. The old name for the district is 'Peakland', appearing in the Anglo-Saxon Chronicles for 924 as 'Peaclond', meaning the land of the hill dwellers. In Saxon times the district lay on the northern edge of the Kingdom of Mercia.
Quite where the demarcation lies between the Dark Peak and the White Peak is a matter of geologically precision, but it lies roughly along the line take by Rushup Edge and the Mam Tor ridge, which separates the limestone of Hope Dale on the south from the dark, weathered sandstone on the north.

2

Dovestone Reservoir

Dovestone Reservoir is immensely popular with visitors from the neighbouring towns. This walk circles it, but then ventures out along a stretch of the Oldham Way.

Total distance: 5½ miles
Start: Binn Green car park along the A635 Holmfirth-Greenfield road. GR018046.

1   Start from the Binn Green car park and go down steps into light woodland to a stile at the bottom. Through the stile, turn left and go down a surfaced lane to the dam of Yeoman Hey Reservoir.

2   Cross the dam and continue on the other side on a broad track, following the shoreline of Dovestone Reservoir and finally turning away from the reservoir towards the in-flowing Chew Brook. There is no need to go down to the bridge over the brook. Instead, branch left onto a contouring vehicle track that cuts across the hillside to meet up with the service track for the much higher and unseen Chew Reservoir.

3   Go up the service track until just past a 'Boundary of Open Country' sign you meet a metal gate and stile, and a bridge spanning an in-flowing stream (Charnel Clough). Immediately after the bridge, leave the service track and descend right, towards Chew Brook.

4   Cross the brook and clamber up steps onto a buttressed level track that offers the easiest of walking, heading back towards Dovestone Reservoir. The path dips at one point to negotiate a stream gully, rising to a stile on the other side, and soon to enter light broadleaved woodland, Chew Piece Plantation.

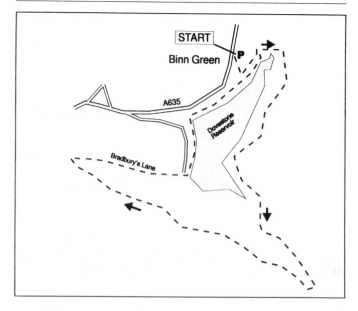

5   Beyond the woodland the track crosses intake pastures and then passes along the top edge of a plantation. Later, trees flank both sides of the path before it reaches a signpost offering a way down to the valley, alongside a stream. Ignore this shortcut, and keep forward, through a gate and once more along a plantation boundary, before finally breaking free.

6   Keep on along the track until you meet the first cottage (on the left), and here turn abruptly right, descending a walled track (Bradbury's Lane). This takes you past a row of old stone-built cottages, where a surfaced lane takes over and leads you out to the car park (and toilets) adjoining the dam of Dovestone Reservoir (there is usually a snack bar here).

7   Cross the dam, and on the other side go through a gate and up a short rising track to a horizontal track hugging the shore of the reservoir. Turn right along this, following it for its full length until it meets a gate giving onto the surfaced lane used at the start of the walk. Turn left and retrace your steps to the Binn Green car park.

3

Yeoman Hey

This is an easy and delightful stroll, good at any time of year, but especially pleasant on a frosty, sunlit day.

Total distance: 4 miles
Start: Binn Green car park along the A635
Holmfirth-Greenfield road. GR018046.

1   As with walks 1 and 2, start from the Binn Green car park and go down steps into light woodland to a stile at the bottom. Through the stile, cross a service lane to a signposted gap in the wall opposite and onto a steadily descending path through light woodland that eventually brings you down to a track above the edge of Dovestone Reservoir.

※   *The area around these Saddleworth reservoirs is very*
※   *much an oasis for the people of Oldham and the surrounding*
※   *conurbation of Greater Manchester. Every weekend will*
※   *see the car parks full to over flowing, and the mobile snack*
※   *bar at the end of the Dovestone Reservoir doing a roaring*
※   *trade. You are unlikely to have the place to yourself at any*
※   *time of year, not even midweek in winter, though this is*
※   *certainly the quietest time.*

2   Go down to and across the dam. On the far side bear left, past the sailing club, and keep following the broad track until in swings left to cross the in-flowing Chew Brook.

3   Turn left with the track and follow it along the eastern shoreline of the reservoir until you reach the dam of the next reservoir to the north, Yeoman Hey.

4   Leave the track before crossing the dam, and branch right onto a signposted footpath that maintains a more or less level course around the steep slopes of Ashway Hey.

5 Just as the dam of Greenfield Reservoir appears, you can follow the path, left, to cross the linking stream by a substantial footbridge. On the other side, bear left, following a track alongside the reservoir until it merges with a slightly higher track.

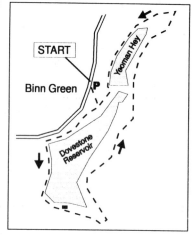

* *The plantation above the Yeoman Hey Reservoir has the curious name Bill o'Jacks. This is a link with a pub that used to be on the A-road above, closed long ago. But in 1832, it attracted a certain measure of notoriety following the murder of the publican, William Bradbury, and his son, Tom o'Bills.*

6 Follow this to the dam of Yeoman Hey, and there turn up a gently rising surfaced track that will take you back to the stile at the bottom of the plantation below the Binn Green car park.

7 Turn into the plantation and ascend the steps back to the start.

The Presence of Man

The Peak, like every other region of Britain, has its record of man's development. But it was the monasteries of the Middle Ages that were the first to make any great use of the region, establishing farming settlements in the valleys and using the moorlands for grazing. Later, large private landowners came, turning their lands to support the increasingly fashionable field sports.

4

Wessenden Head Moor

This splendid moorland walk, flanking the Pennine Way, is ideal in winter or early spring, but do take care not to wander from the tracks and so disturb grouse. There is a great sense of freedom about this area, not something that everyone finds appealing, but it is a lovely place to explore, and little visited except by Pennine Wayfarers, whose trail passes close by.

Total distance: 6 miles
Start: Lay-by on A635. GR077073.

1   Start from a lay-by beside the A635, just east of Wessenden Head Road, and climb the nearby ladder stile to go down a grassy track, soon descending beside a dilapidated wall. Turn left with the track as it heads for the top edge of light woodland. On the far side of the woodland you come onto an old walled track leading to a gate and ladder stile. Over the stile you meet another track at a U-bend.

2   Branch right, descending, here, but only for 80 yards, and then leave the track by climbing a through-stile on the right. Go down the ensuing field, alongside a collapsed wall, and at the bottom corner go through a gap and descend left to cross Marsden Clough by a footbridge.

3   On the other side of the clough, climb a broad track cutting a swathe across the heather moorland of Good Bent, and stay with this as it veers to a south-westerly direction as it heads for a crossing point above Hey Clough.

4   Having crossed the clough, the track rises for a short while alongside another stream and wall before moving away and heading across the moor in a direction north of east. This feeds directly into walled Issues Road, which you now follow for almost a mile until the track bends right.

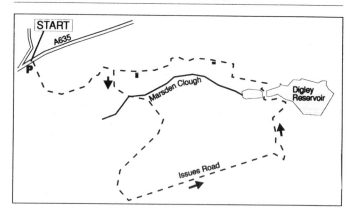

5   About 100 yards before a farmhouse (Meal Hill), branch left onto an obvious track (also walled) that steers you down towards Digley Reservoir. On the way the track is joined from the left by another, and gradually reduces in size to become a muddy path running beside a stream in a narrow gully.

6   At the bottom you meet another path at a T-junction. Turn left and walk beside a wall (on your right) to a gated stile, beyond which a broad path leads on towards another gate and a descent to the dam between Digley Reservoir and its smaller neighbour Bilberry Reservoir.

7 Cross the dam and turn left on the other side, climbing to a gate. After the gate, turn sharp right and walk up a stony walled track to a bench at another track junction. Here turn left, and follow the on-going track as it rises steadily through a right-angled bend and up to another T-junction.

8   Turn left and follow the broad track (Nether Lane), past Greaves Head barns and, later, Goodbent Lodge, an imposing building in a splendid setting.

9   A short way on you meet your outward route and can walk up to the ladder stile ahead, beyond which you simply retrace your steps.

5

Longdendale and Lad's Leap

This exhilarating walk takes a lofty look at the Longdendale valley, sandwiched between the peaty bulk of Bleaklow and Black Hill, before dashing down to the reservoirs to make a leisurely acquaintance with the Longdendale Trail, a popular trans-Pennine walk. There is a sombreness about Longdendale influenced by the underlying gritstone, but in sunlight the landscape comes vibrantly alive, and the area understandably remains one of the most popular places for walkers in the northern Peak.

Total distance: 7 miles
Height gain: 1,050 feet
Start: Crowden car park. GR072993
Type of walk: Quite demanding for young children. A strenuous start, not suitable for misty conditions, followed by easy walking.

Today, the most prominent features in the Longdendale valley are the five reservoirs which, when constructed, comprised the largest expanse of artificial lakes in the world. When full, they are still impressive, and continue to supply water to the Manchester conurbation.

Another invader, from Victorian times, was the Manchester to Sheffield railway, which, further up the valley, burrowed its way through the Pennine hills. The line is now dismantled, but the trackbed is made good use of by walkers and cyclists. During the early part of 2001, there was talk of re-opening this line, re-establishing the direct link between Manchester and Sheffield.

1 Leave the Crowden car park along the path that leads to the toilet block at the nearby campsite, and there turn right to a track junction. Go left, through a gate and on to cross Crowden Brook. A broad, rough track follows, climbing gently to the

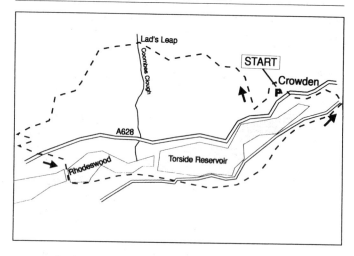

waymarked turning for the Pennine Way. Turn right and continue as far as a ladder-stile.

2   After the stile, turn left and follow the right-hand one of two tracks, which makes its way up the hillside beyond. The ascent becomes quite steep as the path bears left over a collapsed wall towards the top of the hill.

3   After you cross the wall, you continue with another to pass a cairn and waymarker pole, and twice need to deal with a small brook that is either bone dry or clutchingly boggy.

4   Now continue uphill rather less energetically, alongside a wall, and then following an on-going path when the wall ends. Gradually you edge onto the moors above.

The view has already expanded generously, and you begin to realise why this area is a favourite of many. To the south you get good views over Torside Clough onto Bleaklow and the Kinder Plateau beyond. In the valley below, Rhodeswood and Torside Reservoirs, future companions, glisten in the cold light.

5   Almost at the top of the ascent, the wall re-appears, but

your route (and the path) move away from it towards Lad's Leap, following a line of cairns. Two cloughs, Hollins and Coombes meet at Lad's Leap.

6   Whether anyone could leap across at this point is rather debatable; ordinary folk, and those with children, have to content themselves with descending to cross the clough and then walking around the edge of the hill. On the far side turn left, following a path leading downwards across open moor to reach the boundary of Access Land. Here cross Rawkins Brook and climb the right-hand one of two ladder stiles.

7   The path continues down through heather, and passes close by a steep drop into a quarry, Tintwistle Knarr. Keep children under close control here as you go along the edge of a plantation to a stile, and then wind downhill to the A628.

8   Turn left and then, a few strides further on, right through gates down a lane flanked by trees to cross the dam of Rhodeswood Reservoir.

9   On the other side, turn left, up a track, to a stile, and then follow a path along the reservoir until you reach a gate at the dam of Torside Reservoir. Here turn right, onto a rising track, a brief reacquaintance with the Pennine Way, that takes you up to meet a back road.

10 Cross the road with care to join the Longdendale Trail, here parting company with the Pennine Way. Now follow the Trail, which runs along an old railway trackbed, continuing easily for about 2 miles until you can descend sharp left to the back-road again (signposted).

11 Cross into Torside Plantation, following a track through larch plantations to cross above the weir at the outflow from Woodhead Reservoir.

12 On the other side, go steeply left, down a staircase and walk alongside an overflow channel. Follow this until, beyond Crowden youth hostel, you meet another path at a gate. Turn right, and walk up to the A628, and there turn right and soon left to return to the car park.

6

Derwent Edge and the Salt Cellar

Almost any day of the year, Fairholmes, not far from the massive wall of the Derwent Dam, is a natural attraction for visitors, made all the more appealing by some fascinating wood carvings, a battalion of ducks, the chance to spot a goshawk or two, and the fact that you can hire bikes here and tour this delightful valley on two wheels.

But those with a preference for two feet as a mode of transport, will find that, apart from a couple of short uphill sections, this is easy and delightful walking with splendid views of the Derwent Valley – and the uphill bits are not especially demanding.

Total distance: 7 miles
Start: Fairholmes, Derwent Valley.

Modern 'Fairholmes' was originally a farm, and used as a mason's yard during construction of the Derwent and Howden dams between 1901 and 1917. The building of the dams, incomparably awesome engineering structures, demanded the building of their own railway to ferry in supplies of stone from quarries at Grindleford. Equally impressive was the village of dog-legged identical rows of single-storey huts, that sprang up to house the 400 workers involved in work on the dams and their families, more than 1,000 people in all.

Most of the buildings were made of corrugated iron, and earned the village, Birchinlee, the nickname, 'Tin Town', a self-contained settlement, with its own school, canteen, mission, doss-house, post office, village hall and hospital. The village even had its own football team.

Sadly, very little of this purpose-built community now remains. Birchinlee was demolished in or around 1914, and parts of the railway were taken to France and used for transporting troops.

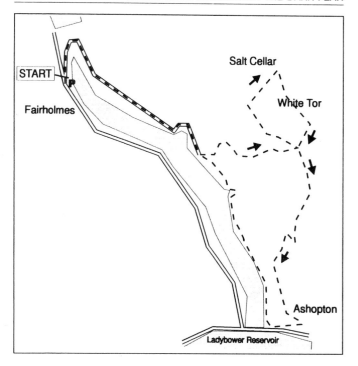

* *The Derwent Reservoir was built, along with the Howden,*
* *to supply water to Derby, Leicester, Nottingham and*
* *Sheffield, and it was used during World War II for training*
* *runs by the famous 617 Squadron, the 'Dambusters',*
* *whose task it was to demolish the Moehne and Eder Dams*
* *in the Ruhr Valley in 1943. Much of the 1955 film, 'The Dam*
* *Busters' was made at Derwent.*

1   From the Fairholmes car park, leave along a path near the
visitor centre (signposted 'Derwent Dam'). Follow a surfaced
track, which soon joins a lane leading towards the reservoir
dam. Following heavy or continuous rain, the dam overflows,
and is an impressive sight.

2   Follow the lane as it curves round to run along the far
side of the northern arm of the Ladybower Reservoir, and

continuing as far as West End, where it ceases to be surfaced.

3   Keep on along the on-going rough track until you reach a bridleway branching left through a gate (signposted 'Via Derwent Edge to Moscar') onto a flagstone path rising obliquely across the hillside and soon curving round to rise to a small group of barns (one with the date 1647).

4   Go through gates onto another path that leads to the stream of Grindle Clough. Cross this and continue beyond on the signposted path for Moscar.

5   Higher up, the path passes through another gate, and then goes up between a wall and a plantation. At the top edge of the plantation another gate gives access to open hill pastures. At one last gate you break free of the intake and meet a track. Turn left (but anyone wanting to shorten the walk can ignore the next section, which simply loops up onto the moors above before returning more or less to the same spot).

6   Having turned left, follow the track until you meet a wall ascending on the right. Leave the track and branch right, climbing alongside the wall to meet one of the Peak District's better known features, the gritstone monolith known as the Salt Cellar. The view from it, along Derwent Edge to Back Tor and across to Kinder and Bleaklow, is sure to sit you down for a while in quiet contemplation.

7   From the Salt Cellar turn right, onto a prominent south-eastbound path along the edge of the moor. This leads you first to another cluster of gritstone boulders, White Tor, just after which you have two choices.

8   Your objective is a meeting of paths at Whinstone Lee Tor. One choice leads you on along the moorland edge, past the Wheel Stones, turning more southerly and then south-westerly and descending to Whinstone Lee Tor. The second choice branches uncertainly down after White Tor, on an intermittent path that takes you back down to the gate you used through earlier. At the gate, turn left, and a short way on, when the path forks, branch right, continuing alongside the intake wall, heading for Whinstone Lee Tor.

9   Arrival at Whinstone Lee Tor from either direction is fairly obvious – a small rounded hillock with a fabulous view. Nearby, a stony track doubles back and descends steeply, right, into Whinstone Lee Fields, a National Trust property.

10 Part way down, bear left to cross a slope to a wall. Continue down beside the wall. The path shortly runs along the top edge of a plantation and then goes forward with trees on both sides, climbing slightly. Eventually the track comes down to a couple of gates.

11 Through the gates, turn immediately right onto a rough vehicle track that goes down to Ding Bank Farm, and then continues beyond. The descending track is surfaced at one point. Leave it at a hairpin bend, by branching right onto the bridleway for Derwent.

12 This track, which runs parallel with the northerly arm of Ladybower Reservoir, can now be followed all the way back to meet your outward route, and then retracing your route back to Fairholmes.

*   *Ladybower was the last of the reservoirs to be built here, between 1935 and 1943, and necessitated the drowning of the villages of Ashopton and Derwent, thirteen farms and numerous small lanes.*
    When the reservoir is very low, some of the foundations of Derwent village are exposed, a poignant sight that many visitors, probably including some former inhabitants, come to marvel at. The original inhabitants of the drowned villages were rehoused at Yorkshire Bridge. When full, the reservoir has a capacity of 6,300 million gallons – some thirst!

7

Derwent Moor Edge

Fine views of the Derwent and Ladybower Reservoirs await on this gentle exploration of the southern edge of Derwent Moor. The walk is ideal for half a day...preferably when the air is clear and the sun warm on your back.

Distance: 3 miles
Start: Lay-by on A57. GR216874.

1   Start from a lay-by along the A57, just east of Cutthroat Bridge. Turn left and walk down to the Bridge, and over it turn right through a gate onto a rising, rocky track that ascends easily into Highshaw Clough.

2   Follow the track as it curves round, rising gently onto moorland, roughly following the line of a post-and-wire fence, until this turn abruptly away, leaving you to continue across heather moorland, with the shapely cone of Winhill Pike away to the left.

3   Gradually, the path rises to a six-way meeting of paths, and here go forward onto a pronounced descending path beside a National Trust sign, into Whinstone Lee Fields estate. The path, rocky underfoot, goes down fairly steeply, with the Derwent Reservoir extending into the blue haze of the Howden Moors.

4   When the track forks, branch left, and descend to walk beside a wall. The track climbs for a while as it passes through a plantation. Eventually it descends through delightful stands of bright green larch to two gates. After the second gate, resume climbing, gently, across brackeny slopes, with Ladybower Reservoir down on your right.

5   Soon the path is accompanied by a wall, and together they

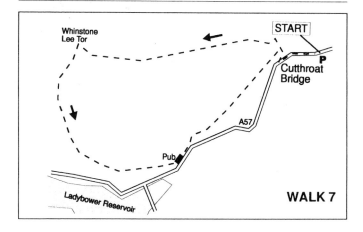

descend to a wooden gate. Beyond, the path continues a little muddily for a while, before descending to pass behind the Ladybower Inn. It then climbs gently once more, as a stony track.

6   The track across the moor eventually brings you down to rejoin your outward route close by Cutthroat Bridge.

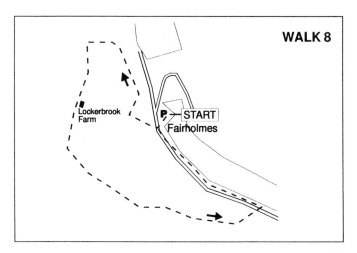

8

West Side Derwent

This moderate walk eases onto the wooded west-side slopes of the Derwent Valley, and has a surprise view in store.

Total distance: 3½ miles
Start: Fairholmes, Derwent Valley.

1   Leave the car park at Fairholmes as if heading out of the valley, but immediately cross the road to go through a wooden gate and onto a concessionary footpath to Lockerbrook.

2   Follow a rising path into plantation, climbing on a stony track that takes you up to a bridge spanning a leat, and continue forward, ascending to meet a higher forest trail, at which you turn left. Keep following the wide forest track (ignore the signposted 'Forest Trail') until eventually it reaches a gate and stile.

3   Turn left onto a broad stony track that takes you down to pass Lockerbrook Farm, beyond which it continues, rising gently along a plantation edge. Keep following the trail until you meet a track junction and a surprise view of the Kinder Plateau and the Mam Tor ridge beyond. Here turn left on a bridleway (signposted: Crookhill Farm) that stays alongside the plantation boundary.

4   The track brings you down to a gate complex at which you should turn left to descend a broad and rough forest trail descending to meet the valley road at the Bridge End car park.

5   As you reach the road, turn right to cross a cattle grid, and immediately left over a stile and onto a grassy (and later gravel) path following the reservoir shore. This eventually emerges back onto the road at another parking space, from which only a short walk beside the road takes you back to Fairholmes.

9

Bridge End Pasture

This agreeable walk zooms through the plantation of Hagg Side, Derwent before enjoying a descending stroll to the reservoir.

Total distance: 4 miles
Start: Bridge End car park.

1   Leave the Bridge End car park along the Derwent Valley road and turn through a wooden gate to begin the ascent of a rough track into the plantation of Hagg Side (signposted: Old Pack Road to Glossop – a clue to its origins). At the top of the plantation you reach a complex of gates, and here turn left to walk along the top boundary of the plantation.

2   The on-going track eventually moves away from the plantation boundary as it heads for a gate and stile, and then continues as a grassy track across open hillside beyond. Go through a gate in a fence, and follow the continuing green path to a gate at which the bridleway forks.

3   Bear left (signposted for Crook Hill Farm and Derwent Valley), still following a green track, and aiming to the left of a hillock ahead (which from this angle conceals Crook Hill). The route becomes waymarked and leads down to run beside a wall, as it heads for Crook Hill Farm. Before reaching the farm, branch left at a signposted footpath to Ladybower (an alternative route that avoids the farmyard), going through a five-bar wooden gate.

4   Bear diagonally right down the ensuing field to a gate in the far right-hand corner. Through the gate cross the farm access to another small gate beside a barn, and in the ensuing field head initially for the Ladybower roadbridge, but soon bearing right to a gate in a wall.

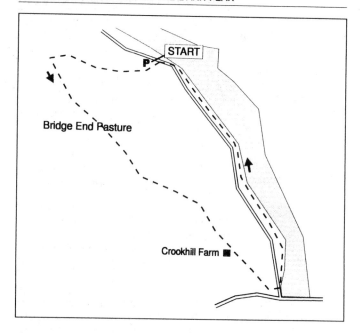

5 Go through the gate and the following ladder-stile onto a descending green path that leads to another stile and gate beyond which the path continues down the middle of the next field. Just after having crossed a stream, go left to meet the valley road.

6 At the road, turn right for a short distance (crossing the road), and then turn sharp left at a stile giving onto a grassy path that parallels the reservoir shore. This path will take you past a reservoir building. Further on, when the path forks, branch right onto a path that stays close to the reservoir edge. The path continues and crosses an in-flowing stream by passing between two large water pipes.

7 A brief scramble up the other side and the path continues easily, almost touching the road at one point, and then easing on towards a stile. As you approach the stile, turn left to the road, cross a cattle grid and return to the Bridge End car park.

10

Yellowslacks and Doctors Gate

The peaty uplands of Bleaklow have been known to make grown men shudder at the thought of them. This walk (which will prove too much for very young children), however, touches on the fringe of this former menace, and makes an ideal outing for a warm summer's day: it should be avoided altogether in anything less than perfect visibility and settled weather.

Total distance: 6 miles
Height gain: 1,445 feet
Start: Shepley Street, Old Glossop. GR046948.

1   The walk begins from the Old Glossop bus terminal at the eastern end of Shepley Street. Here, a broad track sets off beside Shelf Brook, beneath the tree-dotted mound of Shire Hill. Ignore a footbridge when you reach it, but go forward along the continuing bridleway past a farm building. After about 750 yards the track is confronted by a gate. Do not go through the gate, but cross instead a ladder-stile on your left, and ascend between a wall and fence to another stile beyond which the open fellside above Shittern Clough awaits.

2   The on-going path rises steadily, often as a grassy track, but elsewhere rather more boot-worn, until it reaches a top stile. Beyond that a gritstone path probes its way through banks of heather, still rising, but more gently now.

3   Eventually the path becomes of delightful promenade along a level terrace, high above the wall-patterned pastures of the broad-bottomed Yellowslacks valley. The path, at times an intermittent presence, is sandwiched between heather banks on the left and grassy slopes punctuated with gritstone outcrops on the right.

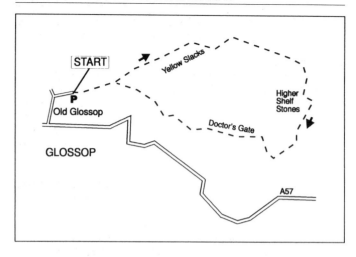

4   In spite of the path's contrary nature, the general direction is never in doubt, you are heading for the narrowing gully down which the infant Yellowslacks Brook carves a course. As it draws near so you encounter a dilapidated fence which escorts you into the narrow confines of Dowstone Clough.

5   Press on with the fence, taking time to admire the view ahead of the knobbly profile of Bleaklow summit and perhaps catch sight or sound of a soaring buzzard or cronking raven. This is a landscape of fine, wide open spaces and rolling hillsides with no hint of the groughy maze that lies ahead.

6   Follow the on-going path into Dowstone Clough. There is always a gentle rise to the route as it follows the streambed until you reach a point where it bends to the right (south), and the path goes with it. Now, suddenly, the landscape is one of peaty hummocks and low gritstone outcrops that in mist is very confusing – hence the advice to go in good weather conditions. The path becomes less distinct and even on a clear day attention needs to be paid to navigation as you try to maintain a southerly course for the sanctuary of Higher Shelf Stones.

7   Gradually the formidable Bleaklow terrain takes over.

When it does, stick as much as possible to the watercourses, many of them dried out and worn through the peat to bedrock.

8   In the end, the peaty groughs surrender their hold as you approach the yellow trig pillar set among the boulders of Higher Shelf Stones. With a sense of relief you gaze across the unseen depths of Crooked Clough to the top of the Snake Pass a little over a mile away to the south, while more prominently the ribbon of the Doctor's Gate path, by which the walk concludes, courses across the lower slopes of Coldharbour Moor.

9   From the trig pillar launch yourself into the grassy, hare-inhabited void between Higher and Lower Shelf Stones, descending into White Clough, and taking great care as you go down. At the bottom of the descent, cross a stream, Shelf Brook, near its confluence with White Clough, and branch right looking for a narrow path that ascends the steep bank ahead to join the Doctor's Gate path.

> *Doctor's Gate is an ancient thoroughfare possibly of Roman origin, linking the forts of Melandra, west of Glossop, with Navio, at Brough, near Castleton. It is thought to be named after Dr. John Talbot, vicar of Glossop between 1494 and 1550, who used the route frequently during the 16th century, though little is known about him. In the 17th century, the road was known as "Doctor Talbotes Gate", while Camden referred to it as Doctor's Gate in 1789.*
>
> *There is also a tradition that Doctor's Gate links Doctor Faustus and the Devil, or that it is a corruption of Dog Tor, in reference to the profile of nearby gritstone boulders, though there are none now that obviously resemble dogs. Modern historians, however, are disposed to the view that Doctor's Gate is simply a medieval packhorse route linking two remote valleys.*

10 Turn right along the path secure in the knowledge that the most trying stages are over and only agreeable walking awaits. At a junction of tracks just after a gate and stile, take the right-hand one of two bridges, following the track out to rejoin the outward route north of Shire Hill.

11

Kinder Downfall

There are few places more renowned than Kinder Downfall, the highest waterfall in the Peak. This walk, which involves quite a bit of ascent, begins from the Bowden Bridge car park, not far from Hayfield and an important place in the history of access in the Peak District.

Total distance: 7½ miles
Height gain: 1,475ft
Start: Bowden Bridge car park. GR048869.

1 From the car park, turn left along Kinder Road, to the grounds of Kinder Reservoir. Here go right, over the River Kinder, and soon leave the road at a gate on the left to follow the riverbank. A few minutes on you rejoin the road.

2 Go through a gate onto a rising path beside a wall. Follow the path around the reservoir to reach the foot of William Clough.

3 Turn into William Clough, climbing steadily and crossing and recrossing the stream, until, when the clough divides, you can branch right to continue the climb to Ashop Head, where you meet the Pennine Way.

4 Turn right onto the Pennine Way, and climb steeply for a while to the edge of the Kinder plateau, and then press on along an obvious path to the Downfall.

5 Cross the shallow River Kinder, and continue south on the Pennine Way to the ravine of Red Brook. (If conditions prevent you from crossing the River Kinder, regrettably you'll need to retrace your steps). Keep on to the trig pillar on Kinder Low.

6 Continue south, passing to the right of Edale Rocks, and descend by a wall to meet an old packhorse route to the

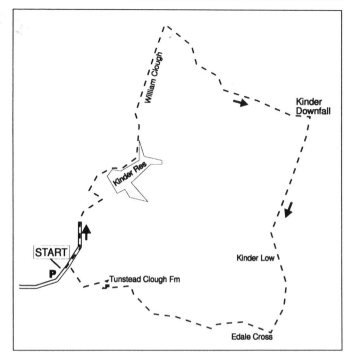

Yorkshire markets from Hayfield and the Sett Valley, near Edale Cross.

7   Return to the valley by heading west from Edale Cross, following the ancient track as far as Oaken Clough and there go right, over a stile, to cross the ensuing hillside, making for Tunstead Clough Farm.

8   Follow the farm access down to the valley bottom. The start is now only a short distance away.

12
Kinder Southern Edges

This is the most demanding walk in this book, and not suitable for very young children. But it will appeal to those with some walking experience already, and to those not so young children now...well, over 50. There are amply opportunities to pause and have a picnic – enjoying the view is one of the essentials of these delightful southern edges of the Kinder plateau.

Distance: 8½ miles
Height gain: 1,460 feet
Start: Edale car park. GR125853.

With little to disturb them but the sound of sheep and the passage of the occasional caravan of packhorses carrying salt to Yorkshire from the mines of Cheshire, and wool on the return trip, the former inhabitants of Edale in Derbyshire must have enjoyed a peaceful, if often arduous, life.

Edale actually comprises five distinct hamlets, each with the suffix 'booth', which signifies 'a temporary shelter for herdsmen' – Nether Booth, Ollerbrook Booth, Grindsbrook Booth, Barber Booth and Upper Booth.

1 From the Edale car park (or the railway station) head up the lane to Grindsbrook Booth where the Pennine Way officially begins (or ends) at the 300-year-old Nags Head Inn. Here turn left (signposted to Upper Booth) to gain a narrow, gently ascending track flanked by stands of hawthorn, holly, rowan, birch and ash, all indicator species of ancient thoroughfares.

2 Shortly, the route, which for half of the journey actually follows the Pennine Way, bears left across a stile, and pursues an uneventful, but very relaxing, route to Upper Booth. From time to time paved sections guide you on, but the way is never in doubt and interrupted only by a succession of stiles.

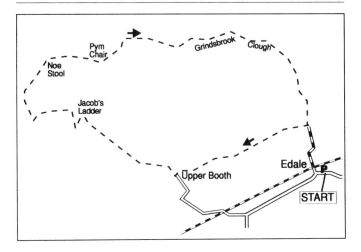

3   At Upper Booth you pass between farm buildings to reach a surfaced lane, there turning right to cross a bridge spanning Crowden Brook before continuing to Lee Farm. Beyond Lee Farm, the valley begins to narrow, as you are brought to the foot of a stepped incline, at Youngit Bridge. The bridge spans the infant River Noe, descending from the Kinder plateau, and is a good place to take a rest before tackling Jacob's Ladder.

Here you are clearly on an ancient packhorse route, and the original line can still be seen setting off left past the remains of a barn before turning again in a sweep that gradually gains height.

The herders who used to control these packhorse trains were called jaggers. One such, Jacob Marshall, who lived nearby at Edalehead House Farm, known locally as Youngit House but now in ruins, used to take a direct line to the top of the hillside so that he could have a few moments to smoke a pipe before his four-legged companions arrived – hence the name, Jacob's Ladder, which is given to the only significant uphill stretch on the whole walk.

4   The state of the Ladder has been improved in recent years, but it is still a bit of a pull, and leads up a rocky track to a gate and wall corner below the rocky upthrust of Swine's Back.

5   As you arrive at the corner, you reach the spot where the outward route ends and you start making your way back, though there's still a little more climbing to do.

6   From the gate and wall corner, turn right onto an ascending track that rises towards Swine's Back, there meeting a prominent path coursing across the hillside. On the way, after three large cairns, the path forks. Here, branch right.

* *All around, the landscape is slashed into peaty groughs that make navigation even in good visibility a nightmare for anyone unwise enough to venture away from the obvious tracks. Everywhere bizarre rock formations protrude from the peat, reminders that these grey gritstone gargoyles have their origins in the sandy water margins of a prehistoric ocean.*
* *The first notable outcrop along the path is Noe Stool, which viewed from its north-eastern side has the likeness of a Toby Jug. A little way on, one outcrop carries the name Pym Chair, another is known as The Pagoda, while yet more, a whole, haphazardly landscaped garden of them, bear the name Wool Packs.*

7   Further on, to one side of the route, Crowden Tower, well worth the detour, commands a fine panorama, but ahead you descend sharply to negotiate Crowden Brook.

8   On escaping the brook, bear slightly right to continue along the edge path, which soon becomes paved. With the conspicuous dome of Grindslow Knoll still quarter of a mile ahead the path forks. Here branch left, to the top of Grindsbrook Clough. A large cairn marks the start of the clough, where you meet the original (and now abandoned) line of the Pennine Way.

9   Go down the clough, it's rocky at the top and wet, but except when the stream is frozen, rarely presents a problem that can't be overcome by a well-placed bottom. Gradually, the clough widens and suddenly you are into the green pastures below Hartshorn and Ringing Roger, steered easily onwards by the path. Nearing Edale, the path descends to a bridge over Grinds Brook, and on the other side climbs to a lane. Turn left, and walk down through the village, back to the start.

13

Rushup Edge

This delightful walk along Rushup Edge is easy to follow and provides stunning views of the Kinder Plateau. After lording it over the Noe Valley for its outward leg, the route then descends into the valley before climbing back to Mam Nick.

Total distance: 5 miles
Start: Mam Nick car park. GR124832.

1   Go up the steps at the rear of the Mam Nick car park and follow a paved path up to meet the road. Turn left onto the road for a short distance and then leave it by branching right on a rising path onto Rushup Edge.

2   Follow the path onto the edge, gaining the narrowest part of the ridge as soon as possible to enjoy the views.

3   Continue along the ridge, passing the high point (Lord's Seat), from where there is a fine retrospective view of the hill-fort on Mam Tor. A wall accompanies you along the ridge, and gradually descends to meet a broad, gravelly track (Chapel Gate).

4   Turn right and follow Chapel Gate down as it slants across the hillside above Whitemoor Clough.

5   At the bottom of the descent, just after a gate/stile, turn left through a gap-stile at the end of a wall, and follow an obvious path across a number of fields to meet the driveway to Manor House Farm.

6   Cross the drive and continue with the on-going path (overgrown at certain times of year) to meet a surfaced lane. Turn right.

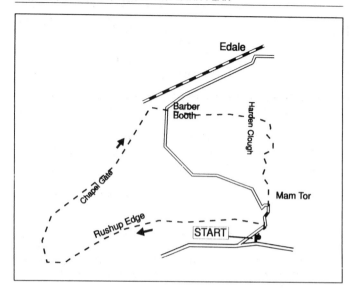

7 At a T-junction, at Barber Booth, go forward onto a rising stony track that soon becomes a broad, field-path leading to a narrow stream gully. Cross this, and follow a waymarked path on the other side until you reach Harden Clough.

8 Turn right as you reach the surfaced track in Harden Clough and follow this to Greenlands Farm. Just at the entrance to the farm, go through a gate on the left, and turn immediately right onto a rising path that will guide you back up to meet the road a short way below Mam Nick.

9 Walk the short distance on the road to cross Mam Nick, and on the other side rejoin your outward route for the short descent back to the car park.

14

Mam Tor

An Iron Age hill-fort and wide-ranging views await visitors who don't mind a bit of uphill work.

Total distance: 3½ miles
Start: Speedwell: old road car park. GR141829.

1   From the car park on the old Mam Tor-Castleton road, cross fields to Speedwell Cavern.

2   Walk up Winnats Pass. (Energetic souls can opt to tackle the steep slope on the right, which climbs steeply high above the pass before descending just as steeply to rejoin the original route. This way, however, would be too demanding for very young children.)

3   Towards the top of the pass, take any of three gates on the right, and turn left alongside a boundary wall to continue climbing, parallel with the road, to Winnats Head Farm.

4   Walk alongside the farm boundary fence to a signpost, and then keep on in the same direction to a stile and across the next field to a road.

5   Cross the road with care and go forward onto Windy Knoll. Take the right branch when the grassy path forks, and follow this to rejoin the road. Again cross with care to a gate diagonally opposite.

6   Climb a broad grassy track leading up to Mam Nick. As you reach the road at Mam Nick, climb right, up steps that take you through the ramparts of Mam Tor's Iron Age hill-fort to the summit.

7   Continue across the summit and down the flagged path on the other side as far as the path junctions at Hollins Cross. (You

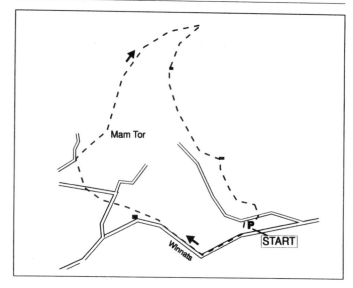

can nip smartly up and down to the neat summit just beyond, if you wish). Then, turn down the right-hand one of two paths, descending south-westwards.

8   When the path forks, keep left to a stile and into a Woodland Conservation Area managed by the National Trust. When you reach a farm access turn right, and immediately after the next farm, turn left over a stile and go down an indistinct grassy path to a gate gap in a fence.

9   Beyond the gap, follow a path across undulating terrain to the site of Odin Mine, reached just beyond a step stile in a fence corner. As you reach the site, turn left on a grassy path descending towards light woodland. Cross another stile and continue descending to Knowlegates Farm.

10 Turn right and follow the farm access out to a road. Turn right to return to the car park.

15

Lose Hill

*The uphill walking to gain the Mam Tor-Lose Hill
ridge is far less demanding than you might
think...and the summit panorama is superb. Save
this walk for a clear day, to enjoy the view.*

**Total distance: 4 miles
Height gain: 1,000 feet
Start: Castleton village centre car park
(Pay and Display).**

1   Leave the car park in Castleton and turn left following the
main road through the village. The road turns sharply left and
then right, but, on the right bend, leave the road by going
forward into a side lane.

2   Follow the lane, which soon runs out into farmland, and
continue until, at a pronounced left bend, you can leave it by
crossing a stile on the right, at the start of a sunken trackway.
This leads onto a path rising clearly to gain the Mam Tor-Lose
Hill ridge at Hollins Cross.

3   At Hollins Cross, turn right and follow the ridge path up and
over Back Tor and on to Lose Hill.

4   From the top of Lose Hill, continue southwards on a
descending flagged path to a stile, beyond which the path
forks. Branch right to another stile, and continue descending
until, just above a farm, you reach a signpost.

5   At the signpost branch right, descending obliquely to a
ladder-stile in a wall corner. Over this, in the ensuing field,
walk to a couple of stiles on the right. After these stiles, cross
the ensuing field to a farm track.

6   Go along the track to a gate, and then continue on a

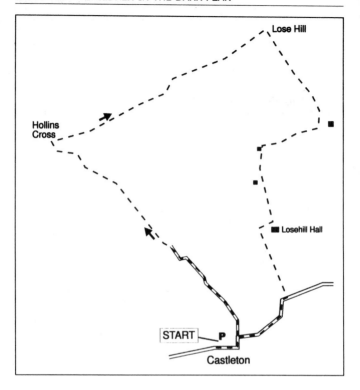

waymarked route along farm tracks and paths back towards Castleton. The path finally descends to a stile giving onto a rough-surfaced track at the rear of Losehill Hall. Turn right.

7   Follow the track around the rear of Losehill Hall and, when it bends left, go down to the road into Castleton, turn right and walk back through Castleton to the start.

16

Around Hope

This agreeable walk, on the boundary between Dark and White Peak, wanders around farm tracks and lanes between Hope and Castleton.

Total distance: 3 miles
Start: Hope car park. GR171835.

1   Leave the car park and turn right. Cross the road and turn left onto a footpath beside Blacksmith's Cottage. Go forward on an obvious path through gates and housing estate. On reaching an estate road, turn right to a T-junction, and there cross to a gate and stile opposite.

2   Through the stile, go forward beside a hedgerow, and follow the signposted path for Lose Hill, maintaining the same direction across a number of fenced enclosures. Cross a railway bridge, and go forward between a house and its outbuildings. After the last of these, keep ahead through a gate and alongside a hedgerow on the right.

3   The path is directed onto a hedged lane and leads to another gate giving into the bottom of a field, across which a path leads to a kissing-gate. Cross the ensuing field to step-stile, but on reaching it, branch left onto a path, which bears left to a gap-stile to the left of a wooden gate. Beyond, follow a green path that heads across the bottom of a sloping field.

4   Cross another stile and maintain the same direction to a waymark beside a footbridge, then head on to another waymark. Cross a second bridge, the onward route, now heading to Spring House Farm, remains obvious throughout and is linked by gates.

5   At a path junction, turn left until, just after the farmhouse, you can turn right onto a broad track. This leads to a lane

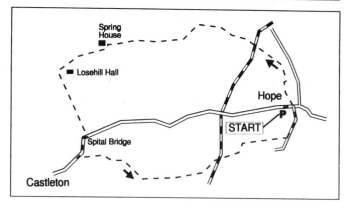

passing to the rear of Losehill Hall. When this bends left, go down to the main road. At the road, turn right, and soon cross Spittal Bridge.

6   150 yards later, turn left at a signposted track to Hope, heading along a walled lane. When the wall ends, continue beside a fence to a stile, at which you enter a large pasture, initially following a fence. When this ends, continue beside a stream on a broad, grassy path. This bears away from the stream to a step-stile in a field corner.

7   Cross the ensuing field to a gap-stile and then go forward through a wall gap and across a narrow field to another stile beside a gate.

8   In the next field, go forward to a waymark, and then keep left of a raised mound beyond which you go slightly left to the far corner, where a stile gives onto a flight of steps leading up to a railway crossing. Cross with great care.

9   On the other side, cross a stile and head along the footpath beyond. The path leads to a road. Turn left and down to Hope. At a T-junction, turn left to return to the car park.

17

Around Hathersage

A pleasant stroll from Hathersage along a peaceful valley, that is an ideal short walk at any time of year.

Total distance: 3½ miles
Parking: Hathersage, near fire station.
GR231814.

* *Hathersage was once the centre of a busy needle and pin*
* *industry, and an important centre for the manufacture of*
* *mill and grindstones, the incomplete remains of which are*
* *scattered about the slopes above the village, notably below*
* *Stanage Edge.*
* *There are also associations with the Brontës here, for*
* *Charlotte is known to have stayed with her lifelong friend*
* *and schoolmate, Ellen Nussey, and is thought to have used*
* *Hathersage as the basis for her fictional town of Morton.*

1   Start from the car park near the fire station in Hathersage and walk towards the main road/village centre. Turn right and walk up to the junction with the B-road that runs up through Dale Bottom, and turn into it.

2   At a bend, a lane goes left towards the church, which is reached up a flight of steps between two houses. When you reach the church, continue past it to a lane at a gate. Turn right.

3   Follow the lane (Baulk Lane), which climbs very gently, until, at a signpost in mid-pasture, it branches half-left to a stile giving onto a path passing behind Brookfield Manor. Continue ahead to a minor road (Birley Lane).

4   Turn left into Birley Lane, and follow this to a junction just beyond Birley Farm. Turn left (Cogger Lane), and continue for

41

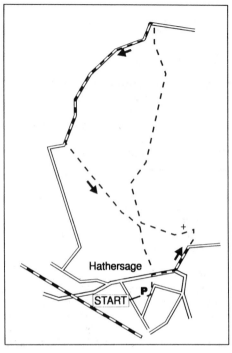

about 400 yards to a stile on the left. Over this, go down a fenced path to a stile, and then continue downhill, keeping left of trees.

5 Cross a drive (private) and keep on to a stream. Cross a bridge and take a path to the right. Go through a stile, and turn immediately left until you reach Baulk Lane once more.

6 Turn right, and follow the lane, past a cricket field, and back to the main road through Hathersage, and cross the road to return to the car park.

North Lees Hall

Sited to the north of Hathersage, an area that would have been familiar to Charlotte Brontë, North Lees Hall, a tall, three-storeyed, castellated tower passed in Walk 18, is said to have provided the setting for Thornfield Hall in Charlotte Brontë's 'Jane Eyre'.
It is presently used as high quality holiday accommodation.

18

Stanage Edge

Leaning over the Hope and Derwent valleys like a wave about to break, Stanage Edge, defines the western edge of Hallam Moors as they clamber indolently from the suburbs of Sheffield, and marks a strong contrast with the lands of the Low Peak. The brief but steep cliffs of the edge are popular with rock climbers, and their antics often a source of entertainment on a warm summer's day.

Total distance: 5½ miles
Height gain: 985ft
Parking: Hathersage, near the fire station in the village centre.

1   On leaving the car park in Hathersage, turn left to the main road. Cross with care and go into Baulk Lane opposite, which degenerates into a broad farm track. The track climbs very gently, until, at a signpost in mid-pasture, it branches half-left to a stile giving onto a path passing behind Brookfield Manor. Continue ahead to a minor road (Birley Lane).

2   Turn right, along Birley Lane until you can go left, uphill, on a track to North Lees Hall, an austere edifice, built by the Eyre family in the 16th century. Pass behind the Hall and ascend a rough flight of steps to a track across a field leading to a small plantation.

3   As you emerge from the plantation onto the old turnpike road that ran from Ashopton to Sheffield, Stanage Edge ranges above you. Turn left, for about 100 yards, and, just before a car park, follow a path on the right, across open pasture, ascending to a small copse directly beneath the rocks of the Edge. From here a path of gritstone blocks leads upwards. This is Jacob's Ladder, thought to be an ancient trod or causeway that has been paved.

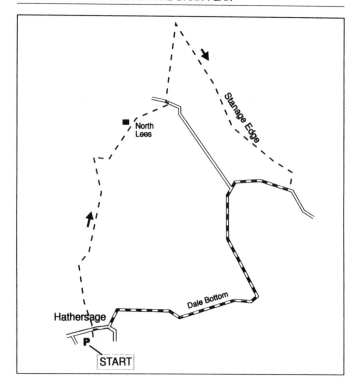

4   Once on the escarpment edge turn right, and follow a path as it traverses to the south-eastern edge of Stanage.

5   The highest point is marked by a trig point. From it you should descend directly to the road over rough ground by any line you are happy with. It is not unduly difficult, but a close watch should be kept on young children while crossing this section.

6   When you reach the road, turn right, and at the next junction, keep left to follow the road through Dale Bottom to the outskirts of Hathersage. At Dale Bottom, turn right to return to the village centre.

19

High Neb

The north-western end of Stanage Edge culminates in High Neb and the shapely rocks of Crow Chin. Along the way there are some fascinating carved bowls in the rocks that may cause puzzlement for a while, until you realise what they are.

Total distance: 4¼ miles
Height gain: 490 feet
Parking: Hollin Bank car park. GR238837.

1 Leave the Hollin Bank car park and turn right until you can climb left across open pasture to a small copse below Stanage Edge. On leaving the shelter of the trees follow a path of gritstone blocks (Jacob's Ladder) that climbs to the escarpment edge.

2 Once on the edge continue north-west (left) with the path, but almost immediately throwing away all the height you have just gained by descending a broad track of loose stones to pass beneath the escarpment of High Neb.

3 Shortly after a wall and stream descending on your right, leave the main track and cross a stile onto a narrower but clear path through bracken. This leads into the midst of a profusion of abandoned millstones, some half carved, others almost complete, but a sad testimony to the end of an important era.

4 Continue on the path through this millstone graveyard, the prominent 'beak' of Crow Chin soaring above you. Onward, the path continues pleasantly, in due course to meet the A57 at Moscar, but long before then you should keep your eyes open for a grassy path ascending, right, through a break in the rock wall, and this by a gentle uphill plod brings you back to the rim of the escarpment a short distance north-west of the trig point on High Neb, the highest point along the Edge.

5 From High Neb follow the edge path on a long and splendid traverse. The scenery is consistently outstanding.

6 When you reach the top of Jacob's Ladder again, turn right and go down it to return to the start by your outward route.

Along the Edge you may notice a series of basins scooped out of the rock, some with curved lines rather like upturned cat's whiskers. All of them are numbered, the first one you will find is 17, though

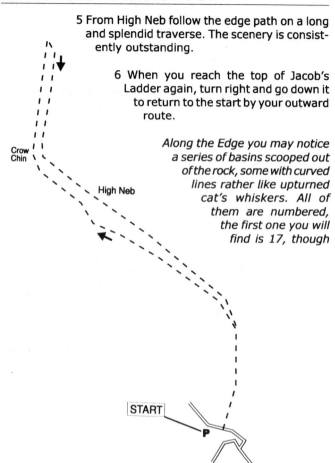

Crow Chin

High Neb

START

P

there are a hundred. They are drinking bowls for grouse, sculpted at the beginning of the 20th century by two gamekeepers who were paid one old penny a time for their construction.

20

Higger Tor and Carl Wark

A trip of endless fascination visiting two hills, one with an Iron Age fort, a spectacular escarpment and waterfalls.

Total distance: 4¼ miles
Parking: Longshaw NT car park. GR267801.

1   Leave the Longshaw (National Trust) car park at its southern end onto a narrow path.

2   Turn right at a junction with a lane and follow signs to Longshaw Visitor Centre. Turn right at the centre and follow a drive to reach a B-road and a footpath on the left leading into woodland. In the wood, when the path forks, branch right to the main road, immediately opposite a track known as the Duke of Rutland's Drive.

3   Cross the road (with care) and follow the drive, an old green road through rocky terrain, below Burbage Rocks to Upper Burbage Bridge at a moorland road.

4   Turn left and cross the bridge. Leave the road, left, onto the higher of two paths heading for Higger Tor, a small gritstone hill, and a good place for a breather.

❋   *'Higger Tor' may well be a corruption of 'higher', though it*
❋   *may be connected with some prehistoric God. In spite of its*
❋   *modest height it commands an extensive panorama.*

5   Carl Wark protrudes from heather and bracken, through which a path weaves a way to an easy climb onto this second rocky tor, the summit of which is though to be an Iron Age hill-fort.

❋   *Carl Wark is a natural fortress, a flat-topped hillock with a*
❋   *ready-made defensive wall of cliffs. It was natural that our*

prehistoric ancestors should chose such a site to build a hill-fort. For some time it was thought to date from the Iron Age, but modern opinion suggests that it is of later construction.

6   A path descends from the south-western edge of Carl Wark through bracken. Eventually it reaches the A-road.

7   Cross the road and follow a path into woodland and across Burbage Brook, passing some attractive waterfalls on the way. Keep forward through the woods to meet the B6521. Turn right, but soon leave the road down a drive to Longshaw Visitor Centre.

8   From the Visitor Centre retrace outward route to the car park.

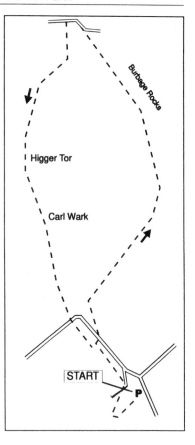

Guide
Pu|

C000219127

Laurie Page

COUNTRYSIDE BOOKS
NEWBURY BERKSHIRE

First published 2017
© Laurie Page 2017
Reprinted 2020

COUNTRYSIDE BOOKS
3 Catherine Road
Newbury, Berkshire

To view our complete range of books,
please visit us at
www.countrysidebooks.co.uk

ISBN 978 1 84674 345 0

Photographs by Laurie Page
Photographs of Cotton and Yoxford by Mark Mitchels
Cover design by Barrie Appleby

Designed by KT Designs, St Helens
Produced through The Letterworks Ltd., Reading
Typeset by KT Designs, St Helens
Printed in Poland

Introduction

The writing of this book encouraged me to move to Suffolk from Essex, the county of my birth. After more frequent visits, my decision was made and so now I live here, in an old Tudor house a stone's throw from the countryside and the River Stour. The appeal of Suffolk is obvious, some lovely old historic towns such as Lavenham and Bury St Edmunds, wonderful rolling countryside, an enticing coastline and many pretty villages, most of them with a pub. There is an abundance of hostelries in the county, and they are often the hub of the village where communities and visitors gather for a meal, a drink and a chat. Some towns have many pubs, such as Long Melford, where I chose the Black Lion, but there were six others to choose from! I have opted mostly for the sort of spot that ramblers like most, a homely inn with character, old beams, comfy chairs and an inglenook fireplace with a log fire on colder days. I hope you enjoy these walks as much as I have. I had fun devising the routes, taking the photographs and drawing the maps. I look forward to visiting more little villages and interesting Suffolk places with my wife, Deborah, who accompanied me on many of these walks.

Publisher's Note

We hope that you obtain considerable enjoyment from this book; great care has been taken in its preparation. However, changes of landlord and actual pub closures are sadly not uncommon. Likewise, although at the time of publication all routes followed public rights of way or permitted paths, diversion orders can be made and permissions withdrawn.

We cannot, of course, be held responsible for such diversion orders and any inaccuracies in the text which result from these or any other changes to the routes, nor any damage which might result from walkers trespassing on private property. We are anxious though that all details covering the walks and the pubs are kept up to date and would therefore welcome information from readers which would be relevant to future editions.

Guide to Suffolk Pub Walks

The simple sketch maps that accompany the walks in this book are based on notes made by the author whilst checking out the routes on the ground. However, for the benefit of a proper map, we do recommend that you purchase the relevant Ordnance Survey sheet covering your walk.

To get in touch visit our website: www.countrysidebooks.co.uk

Queen's Head, Blyford

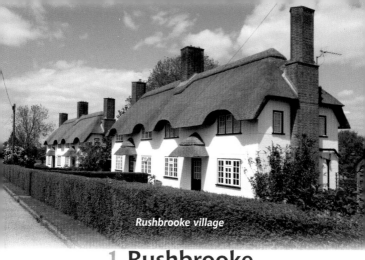

Rushbrooke village

1 Rushbrooke

4 miles (6.4 km)

WALK HIGHLIGHTS

This walk reveals some lovely countryside views, a pretty village and lots of interesting things to see on the way. Not to mention a good pub for refreshment at the end of the walk. Although there is some road walking, these are quiet country lanes. Look out for the 19th-century water pump housed in a small 16th-century building between some very pretty thatched cottages.

THE PUB

The Rushbrooke Arms www.eating-inn.co.uk
☎ 01284 388242 **IP30 0BU**

THE WALK

1 The start of the footpath runs from the side of the pub where the children's play area is. Go uphill and at the fence line by the trees, turn right on the other side of the fence, along a wide grass strip on the field edge. This is part of St Edmund Way. At the end, go almost straight over,

5

HOW TO GET THERE: The Rushbrooke Arms lies directly on the A134 two miles south of Bury St Edmunds where the River Lark crosses the road. **Postcode** IP30 0BU

MAP: OS Explorer: 211 Bury St Edmunds & Stowmarket

PARKING: The pub is happy for walkers to leave their car in the car park while they go for their walk.

to the right of a high fence along a narrow path. Then follow the post and rail fence to the lane. Cross over and go through a wooden gate and into a pretty meadow with trees.

The footpath continues as a wide avenue between trees and soon you are on the old dismantled railway line raised above the landscape with a steep drop on either side. Go uphill then back down and just before a little bridge, take the stile on the left; the path goes left again on the other side, going uphill. The path curves right and follows a hedge of

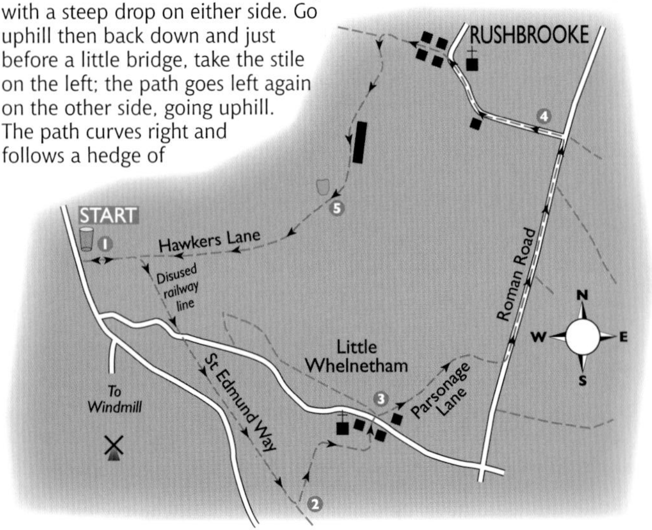

RUSHBROOKE

START

Hawkers Lane

Disused railway line

To Windmill

St. Edmund Way

Little Whelnetham

Parsonage Lane

Roman Road

hawthorn. There are good views to the left and the white gleaming tower in the far distance is the St Edmundsbury Cathedral in Bury St Edmunds. Before the end of the field, a yellow footpath arrow sends you right with more distant views. The path bends sharp left past cottages to the road.

③ Turn right then immediately left along the byway. Continue all the way to the end of this shady path, which gets narrower towards the end. When you reach the lane, turn left along a very straight road. There is a good reason for this; it is a Roman road. Continue along this quiet lane for over half a mile to a road junction. Here you turn left signposted to Rushbrooke.

④ Continue up the lane towards the little church of St Nicholas Rushbrooke. After you pass the church, where the lane bends right, turn left along the footpath taking you to an unusual building which houses the village water pump. Just past this are pretty thatched cottages. As the concrete track deviates to the right, turn left where you will see a footpath way-marker post. Take the footpath that follows the track. There is open farmland to the right.

⑤ After some distance you reach a little T-junction of tracks where you turn right and pass a pond. Where the track swings to the right, go straight on along a grass path. After a while you will see the cathedral tower come into view again in the distance to your right. Cross a track and follow a shady path between the trees. Then you descend back down to the path you came up and the Rushbrooke Arms.

PLACES OF INTEREST NEARBY

If you drive along the main road just two miles north of the pub, you will arrive at **Bury St Edmunds**, a favourite Suffolk town. There is much to see here but the highlight of course is Suffolk's only cathedral and the abbey gardens. The abbey gate dominates the main street. Parts of the cathedral are open to the public. The Crypt Treasury holds exhibitions and visitors can see books from its ancient library. There are too many other places to visit to be specific here, but they include **Greene King Brewery**, ancient buildings, picture galleries, museums and restaurants.

2 Whepstead

3 miles (5 km)

WALK HIGHLIGHTS

Once the property of Bury Abbey, Whepstead, became a possession of the Drury family at the Dissolution of the Monasteries in the 16th century. Whepstead's 13th-century church is dedicated to St Petronilla, the only such dedication in England. Today this village is rather quieter, with just the church, a pub and a village hall. The pub dates from the 17th century and won a tripadvisor Certificate of Excellence in 2015.

THE PUB

The White Horse www.whitehorsewhepstead.co.uk
☎ 01284 735760 **IP29 4SS**

THE WALK

1 From the pub car park, turn right along the lane. Go downhill and at the bottom of the hill, take the footpath on the left across the wooden bridge and along the field edge next to the stream. After the path bends left, follow the way-marker, going straight on across the crop field. When

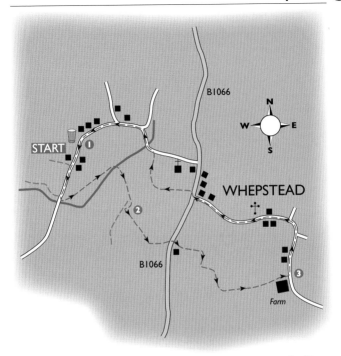

HOW TO GET THERE: Whepstead is situated about 4 miles south of Bury St Edmunds. From the A143 between Bury St Edmunds and Haverhill, take the B1066 south and after 3 miles you reach the village. Turn into Church Hill and at the end bear left into Rede Road where you will find the White Horse pub. **Postcode** IP29 4SS

MAP: OS Explorer 211 Bury St Edmunds & Stowmarket

PARKING: You are welcome to use the pub car park if you are visiting the pub.

you reach the other side, cross a ditch via a little planked bridge and bear right around the field boundary. Continue following the way-makers and at the footpath junction turn right over another wooden bridge.

2 Proceed alongside a large field. In the far corner go left over the next bridge then right, following the field boundary. Then head very gently uphill, eventually reaching a road. Take the footpath opposite which goes right along the field edge then swings left at the corner. The path bends left then right, then up along a narrow stretch between a hedge and a fence. At the end of the field go through the gap in the hedge and turn left along a wide grass path with a hedge to your left. Proceed straight on, where the path continues through shrub, then alongside horse paddocks to the road.

3 Turn left. At the next road junction, continue straight on up the road (Mickley Green) and later join a pavement, passing houses, the Baptist Chapel and The Old Rectory. At the road T-junction turn right and almost immediately, take the next footpath on the left. Go down past a large oak with good views ahead. The path bends right and eventually emerges at the lane. Turn left then left again at the next road junction. Continue past Old School Road and back to the White Horse pub.

PLACES OF INTEREST NEARBY

Just a few miles north of Whepstead, just off the A143, is the grand National Trust property of **Ickworth House** with its rotunda, extensive gardens and parkland. The building of the house started in 1795 and was the creation of the 4th Earl of Bristol, who is buried in Ickworth church within the grounds. Inside the rotunda are many important works of art by famous artists and a magnificent collection of Georgian silver. The east wing is now a hotel. www.nationaltrust.org.uk/ickworth

3 Preston St Mary

3.2 miles (5.2 km)

WALK HIGHLIGHTS
If you like a 'get away from it all' walk, this route around the quiet village of Preston will be just right. In 2016, the pub was voted Suffolk's best pub restaurant by the *Suffolk Life* publication. The walk takes you through some remote countryside with lovely rural scenery to the little hamlet of Kettlebaston.

THE PUB
The Six Bells www.thesixbellspreston.com
☎ 01787 247440 **CO10 9NG**

THE WALK
1 From the pub entrance, turn right along the village street following the little walkway. Turn left up Church Lane. Go through the church gate (the church is usually open to visitors) and from the churchyard you can leave by the little wooden gate taking you back out into Church Lane. Continue along the concrete track going gently downhill with good

Guide to Suffolk Pub Walks

HOW TO GET THERE: From Lavenham, Preston St Mary is signed and after about 2 miles at the fork turn right into the village. The pub is further down on the right. **Postcode** CO10 9NG

MAP: OS Explorer 211, Bury St Edmunds & Stowmarket

PARKING: Providing you use the pub the owner is quite happy for you to use the pub car park. There is a small area in front of the pub and a car park at the rear.

countryside views ahead. At the end, go through the gate just to the left and proceed along a grass path which bends left by the stream. Then cross the stream via the wooden footbridge and a gate.

② Go through the next gate opposite and proceed straight on uphill between the ditch and hedge on the left and the fence on the right. At the end go through two more gates either side of the farm access drive and on to the lane. Turn right along the lane. Proceed along the

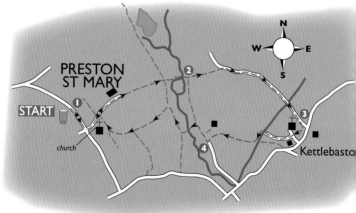

winding lane for some distance until you reach the pretty little hamlet of Kettlebaston. Turn right opposite Church Farm, taking you to the parish church of St Mary the Virgin, also open for a visit.

Continue straight on past the church and into a wooded area with a horse paddock to the left. At Hall Yard go straight on through a wooden gate (to the right of the large black gate). Follow the tarmac path all the way down to the brook where you turn left on the other side of the brook through a wooden gate. Continue between the brook and the fence. Swing right at the footpath junction and proceed uphill. At the top negotiate two more wooden gates, going straight on then down to where the path swings left. At the end you are guided down steps to a stony path.

Turn right and proceed straight ahead along a grass path alongside a brook. Go left at the wooden fingerpost, passing a pond to your right. Cross a wooden bridge over the stream. Continue through a crop field and at the end by the hedge, turn right along a wide grass path. Where the hedge on your left ends, turn left over a little planked bridge and up along the field boundary with a hedge on the right. At the end of the field go through the gap in the corner (there is a seat for a rest) and then bear left heading for the church you see ahead. Follow the path to the end where you emerge back onto Church Lane, Turn left and retrace your steps into the village and to the Six Bells pub.

PLACES OF INTEREST NEARBY

Just 3 miles south is the wonderful town of **Lavenham**. With about 340 listed buildings, it is an amazing example of an English medieval town. Highlights include the 16th-century **Guildhall** which is open to the public and has had a variety of functions over the years. There is also the museum in **The Little Hall**, a large antiques centre and the **Angel Gallery**, a 15th-century wool merchant's house now containing an art collection. There are many good pubs and restaurants.

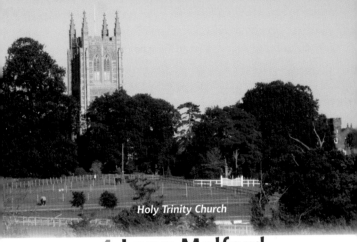
Holy Trinity Church

4 Long Melford
4.5 miles (7.2 km)

WALK HIGHLIGHTS
Long Melford is a delightful ancient village which thrived in the middle ages as a wool town. The main street is made up of interesting houses, shops and antique emporiums (made famous by the filming of the TV show *Lovejoy*). You also pass the magnificent Kentwell Hall at the start of this walk.

THE PUB
The Black Lion www.blacklionhotel.net
☎ 01787 312356 **CO10 9DN**

THE WALK
1. From the pub, head up Church Walk to the end and into the church grounds. Steer to the left of the church via the path and exit the churchyard by the side gate. Go over a stile and soon after on the right go through an unusual metal gate and across a small meadow, then through the trees to a stile. This brings you to a large open meadow where sheep graze. Go

HOW TO GET THERE: Long Melford is just north of Sudbury. The Black Lion is on the junction between the B1064 from Sudbury and the A1092 just north of the village. **Postcode** CO10 9DN

MAP: OS Explorer 196 Sudbury.

PARKING: There is a parking area overlooking the green just off Church Walk near the pub.

right to a stile and turn left onto the wide beech tree-lined drive leading to Kentwell Hall. Just before the gates of Kentwell Hall veer left along a wide unmade track.

Walk through a wooded area then pass through a wooden gate. Towards the end,

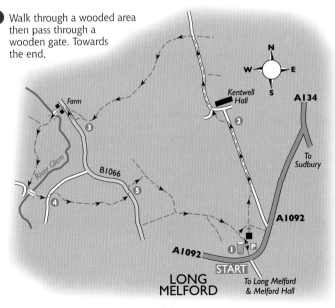

before you reach the next wooden gate, go right on an unsigned path through a meadow, then another metal pedestrian gate and continue straight on up the track. Pass another wood on the left and soon after, at a little track junction, look out for a footpath post going left. Follow this grass path along the edge of two large fields. At the footpath post veer right, straight across the field on a narrow path. At the bottom of the field cross a wooden bridge. Continue on through the farm, to the right of the silos, to the road.

3 Turn right along the road, keeping to the raised grass verge. At Mill Barn go left down the bank and along the Stour Valley footpath opposite, between buildings and fences. Cross a narrow bridge and bear right through the field. Cross the bridge and continue straight on uphill. Follow the arrows into a large field with a hedge on your left. When you reach the ditch go left, then almost immediately right across the ditch, and across the field. Head directly for the bungalow on the other side of the field. Then continue straight on along the track past the cottage. Turn left into the entrance of Sluice Gate Cottage and cross the bridge over the River Glem. Proceed through a thicket and a field to the lane.

4 Turn left and just past Parsonage Farm, take the footpath on the right by the wood. You are guided left over planks and then uphill. The church can soon be seen ahead. Where the hedge ends, go straight on through a field. At a sign by the road, turn left and almost immediately, take the footpath on the right through a field.

5 At the oak tree by a footpath post go straight on across a field. At the T-junction in the middle of the field, turn right to a way-marker post at the edge and cross wooden planks following the field edge with a hedge to the right. The path eventually crosses the ditch by a culvert to a path junction. Take the left option and head towards the church. Continue straight on along the edge of the horse paddocks. Cross two stiles to re-trace your steps to Church Walk and the Black Lion pub.

PLACES OF INTEREST NEARBY

There are two magnificent stately homes in Long Melford: **Kentwell Hall** and the National Trust's **Melford Hall**. www.kentwell.co.uk and www.naanationaltrust.org.co.uk/melfordhall

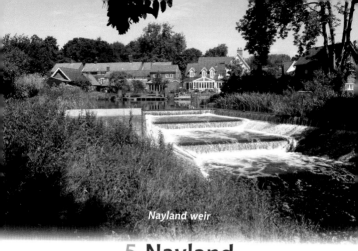

Nayland weir

5 Nayland
4 miles (6.4 km)

WALK HIGHLIGHTS
Nayland is historically a small market town. It appears in the Domesday Book and adjacent to the pub is Court Knoll, a site dating back to Norman times. Today, many old half-timbered and gabled buildings have remained in the village. The route follows footpaths by the banks of the River Stour, passing meadows, woods and farmland.

THE PUB
The Anchor Inn www.anchornayland.co.uk
☎ 01206 262313 **CO6 4JL**

THE WALK
1 Take the footpath on the other side of the road from the pub, by the Horkesley Road sign on the bridge, going down the steps. Follow the path along the pretty meandering river past the weir. Continue between a lake and the river and on up a steep bank to the main road. Turn right along the main road for a short distance. Cross over the main road at

17

Guide to Suffolk Pub Walks

HOW TO GET THERE: You can reach Nayland from the A134 between Colchester and Sudbury. The next road, just south of the junction with the A134 and the B1087 which runs through the village, is Horkesley Road which leads directly to the pub in Court Street, on the other side of the bridge. **Postcode CO6 4JL**

MAP: OS Explorer 196 Sudbury, Hadleigh & Dedham Vale.

PARKING: There is limited parking at the pub but a spot can usually be found further along Court Street.

the next junction at Nags Corner and turn left into Wiston Road. Almost immediately, take the footpath on the left through the wooden kissing gate.

2 The footpath follows the edge of two successive fields, both with a wire fence on the left. Cross a wooden bridge and stile and carry on through shrub, then a meadow and over another bridge, and alongside a crop field. At the way-marker post, continue on a long straight path. After some distance you pass Wiston Mill house on the left. When you reach the next footpath

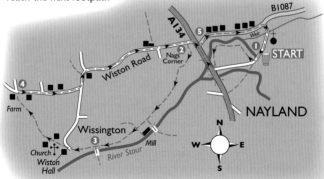

junction, do not cross the bridge but keep to the same side of the stream.

3 As you approach Wiston Hall keep to the right. The footpath bends right then left, taking you to the little parish church of St Mary the Virgin which usually remains open. The path runs through the churchyard to the right of the church and you leave through a gap in the wall at the other end. Go through a kissing gate and across the meadow. Keep to the left then pass through a kissing gate into a wood on a winding and undulating path. You emerge out of the wood via a stile into an open field. Continue alongside the fence and over another stile to a wide track. Turn right up the track to the lane by Rushbank Farm.

4 Turn right along the lane. This is a quiet road but nevertheless watch out for traffic as there is not always a good verge. Pass The Old Maltings. The lane turns sharp left then at the next road junction, go right along Wiston Road signposted to Nayland. Continue for ¾ mile, passing Little Bulmer Farm to the end of the lane. The last section has a good pavement.

5 At the road junction you may wish to turn right and retrace your steps by the river, but to see more of the village cross the main road and go straight on taking you past more modern residences at first, and then some quaint old cottages. Follow the road as it swings right into the High Street. The church soon comes into view and you pass shops and more interesting old buildings. The Anchor is at the end of the village on the left.

PLACES OF INTEREST NEARBY

Nayland is about 8 miles south of Sudbury and less than 8 miles north of Colchester, in Essex. For art lovers Sudbury is the birth place of Thomas Gainsborough. **Gainsborough's House** is a museum and gallery exhibiting some of his paintings. ☎ 01787 372958
www.gainsborough.org
Colchester Castle is a splendid Norman castle and museum open to the public. Guided tours are available. ☎ 01206 282939
www.cimuseums.org.uk

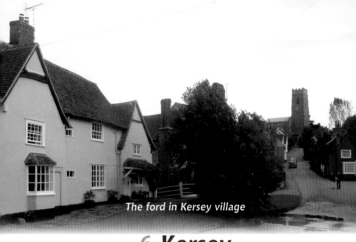

The ford in Kersey village

6 Kersey
3.8 miles (6.2 km)

WALK HIGHLIGHTS
Kersey is undoubtedly one of the prettiest villages in Suffolk and is well known for the ford that runs through its centre. There are colourful cottages, and a well-regarded, timber-framed pub dating back to 1379. Despite the few lanes and roads on this route there is very little in the way of traffic.

THE PUB
The Bell Inn www.kerseybell.co.uk
☎ 01473 823229 **IP7 6DY**

THE WALK
1 From the Bell turn right, going downhill and over the ford via the footbridge on the left. At the next road junction go right, past Market House and immediately right again through a wooden gate between the half-timbered buildings. Then through another gate, over a stile and alongside a field. After the next stile go straight on and continue for some distance between the brook and the fence. Eventually, you pass

HOW TO GET THERE: Take the A1141 just north of Hadleigh and Kersey village is signposted to the west, or from the south on the A1071. **Postcode** IP7 6DY

MAP: OS Explorer 196 Sudbury, Hadleigh & Dedham Vale.

PARKING: The Bell Inn has a car park but check with the landlord first.

through a gate on the left then continue in the same direction along the edge of a hilly grass field to the corner, at a double stile and a bridge crossing the brook. Bear slightly left towards the ruined building and, to the left of it, go through two metal gates, following the arrows up a wide track. This soon bends right going uphill to Bridges Farm.

② Go through the farm buildings and up the little lane. Continue all the way

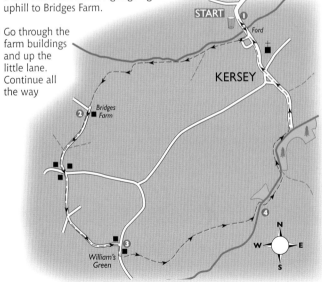

to the end, to the road junction where you turn left then immediately right following the 'By Road' sign along a lane bordered by high hedges. At the crossroads go straight over, still following the By Road. Pass some cottages and proceed to the 1937 commemoration tree, then continue to the T-junction at William's Green where you turn right and soon after, just on the other side of Old Mill House, take the footpath on the left.

3 Follow the track, then keep left alongside the field edge with a dense hedge on your left. There is some lovely open countryside with distant views. The path bends left in a large arc, and just after the end of the bend look out for a fallen way-marker post taking you left up a little bank and into a small wood. You soon emerge into a large field with a wide grass path and a high hedge to your right. Continue gently downhill to the end of the field. When you reach the far corner, bear slightly right following the wooden footpath sign. Kersey church can be seen in the distance. As the hedge and the grass path ends, go straight on over the middle of the crop field, dropping down to a marker post at the bottom by the stream.

4 Turn left. Follow the line of the brook and just before the corner of the field, turn right crossing the stream via a wooden bridge. Then up the wooden steps and turn left. Continue gently down past the cottage and at the very end turn left, on the other side of the hedge across a stile and bridge, then right along the concrete track. This later bends sharp right and follows the brook. Then walk uphill, with enjoyable views to your right. Keep left at the road junction, pass houses and contiune to a huge oak with seats underneath. Turn right along the road then left at the next junction soon after, taking you to Kersey Street and past the church. Go back downhill to the ford and the pub.

PLACES OF INTEREST NEARBY

Five minutes' drive to the south-east is the town of **Hadleigh**. It has an unusually long main street with colourful old buildings. Other points of interest include a medieval bridge, Deanery Tower, a 15th-century gatehouse and a medieval guildhall.

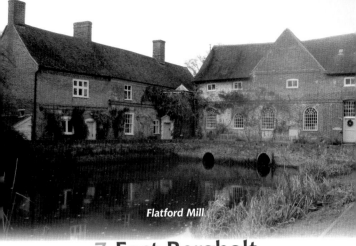

Flatford Mill

7 East Bergholt

4 miles (6.5 km)

WALK HIGHLIGHTS

The village of East Bergholt is associated with John Constable, the famous artist who was born here in 1776. You pass both Flatford Mill and Willy Lott's Cottage, which featured in his masterpiece *The Hay Wain*.

THE PUB

The Red Lion (no website but there are various reviews on tripadvisor and suffolkcamra.co.uk)
☎ 01206 298332 **CO7 6TB**

THE WALK

① From the car park, turn right along the road, past the Red Lion to the first junction by the post office where you turn right again, along a little lane that runs past the Congregational Church. Continue to the gate to Vale Farm, where you take a footpath to the left going down to a wooden footbridge across the brook. Continue straight on going back uphill. At the top you emerge into an open field with views to the left of Dedham

Guide to Suffolk Pub Walks

HOW TO GET THERE: East Bergholt can be reached by turning off the A12 onto the B1070 which takes you into the village. Turn into Gaston Street and the Red Lion is at the end, in the heart of the village. **Postcode** CO7 6TB

MAP: OS Explorer 196 Sudbury, Hadleigh & Dedham Vale.

PARKING: There is a large free public car park directly behind the pub.

church and the surrounding countryside. At the end of the field at the footpath junction turn left down a shady tree-lined path. At the bottom, just before the metal gate, turn left.

2 Continue for some distance winding between the trees. When you reach a planked bridge and stile, bear left through a grass field. Cross another stile to follow a narrow path by a barbed wire fence. Negotiate another stile and immediately swing left to the next stile by the house. Turn right along a wide track. You cross a bridge and soon after reach a more substantial bridge where you cross the River Stour.

3 You are now on the Essex side of the river. Bear slightly right on the path that runs across the field to the culvert that crosses a stream and continue through the meadow with the River Stour to your left on the path that runs parallel. You merge closer to the river further along. At the next bridge, cross back over the river and at the 16th-century Bridge Cottage, turn right. Continue to the end of the lane, passing the Granary, the Flatford Mill Field Centre and the famous Willy Lott's Cottage, where you reach an information board.

4 At the path junction after Willy Lott's Cottage, turn left by the board along the track, part of the Stour Valley path. Where the footpath bends right, go straight on through a kissing gate onto a permissive route and bear left, following a wide grass path that swings left and goes uphill. At the top by the bench, go straight on through another gate and gently up along the field edge. Proceed straight on to where the path narrows between fences. At the path T-junction turn left and soon after, go through a wooden gate, joining an access road which leads down to the lane.

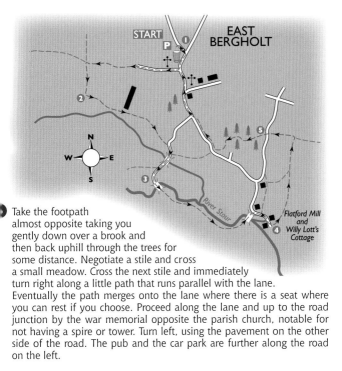

Take the footpath
almost opposite taking you
gently down over a brook and
then back uphill through the trees for
some distance. Negotiate a stile and cross
a small meadow. Cross the next stile and immediately
turn right along a little path that runs parallel with the lane.
Eventually the path merges onto the lane where there is a seat where
you can rest if you choose. Proceed along the lane and up to the road
junction by the war memorial opposite the parish church, notable for
not having a spire or tower. Turn left, using the pavement on the other
side of the road. The pub and the car park are further along the road
on the left.

PLACES OF INTEREST NEARBY

The famous **Flatford Mill**, once owned by John Constable's father, has
a visitor centre providing a history of the family. The **John Constable
Museum** at Bridge Cottage is also worth a look and has free admission.
www.nationaltrust.org.uk/flatford-bridge-cottage

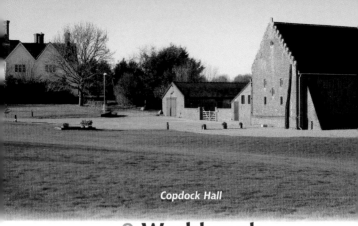

Copdock Hall

8 Washbrook

5 miles (8.1 km)

WALK HIGHLIGHTS
Quiet and peaceful countryside a stone's throw from the bustle of Suffolk's largest city, Ipswich. Some agility and energy is required as there are no fewer than 16 stiles. Look out for Copdock Hall, a Grade II listed brick barn.

THE PUB
The Brook Inn www.thebrookinnwashbrook.co.uk
☎ 01473 730531 **IP8 3HR**

THE WALK
1 The footpath runs between fences by the pub car park. Cross a stile and walk uphill. Cross a stile then follow the hedge to the corner of the field. Over another stile then straight on by a wire fence. Cross a stile and brook then another stile to a track. Go up steps and over a stile into a field. Go straight ahead under pylons and head for where the line of the hedge ends. Take the footpath over the stile on the left into a field. Keep to

26

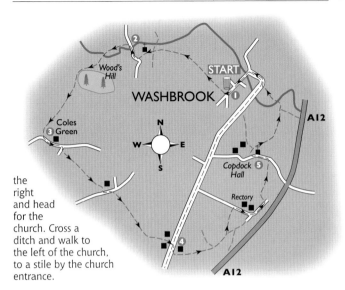

the
right
and head
for the
church. Cross a
ditch and walk to
the left of the church,
to a stile by the church
entrance.

At the church veer left between fences to the lane and turn right. Cross a stream, then left over a stile onto the footpath. Look out for a footpath post directing you left before you reach the iron gates ahead. Cross a stream via a little planked bridge and bear right, up to another footpath

HOW TO GET THERE: Washbrook is easily reached from the A12. The B1113 runs directly into the village from the north and access from the south is via the A12 junction before the Ipswich roundabout. **Postcode** IP8 3HR

MAP: OS Explorer 197 Ipswich, Felixstowe & Harwich.

PARKING: If you visit the pub check with the landlord before leaving your car. Alternatively park roadside nearby.

post directing you into the next field and around the wood. The path curves left over a stile by an iron gate and through a valley. Continue between hedges, then by a field with a hedge to the left. Keep to the right of the next hedge to the road.

3 Turn left and pass Coles Green Farm. At the pink cottages turn right then immediately left through a gate. Bear left around the allotment and through two more gates into a field. Follow the wooden fence then fork left through trees. Cross a stile and a field to another stile. Turn left along the lane and just past the red brick house, take the footpath on the right. Bear slightly left. The path runs between two fields and under pylons. Dip down into the next field. The path bends left. Continue to the road at Elm Farm House.

4 Turn right along the dual carriageway, then cross at Tom Cat Farm and take the footpath opposite by Copdock House. At the end of the fence bear slightly left across the field. Pass through two hedgerows and immediately after the second, go diagonally left across the field. Cross the next field, over a ditch into the next field between fences and onto a track. Turn right passing the Old Rectory. At the T-junction turn left. Take the next footpath on the left through a kissing gate and onto a track which bends right. Keep to the right and continue over a stile. Go through a kissing gate. At the next lane turn left into the churchyard.

5 Pass the church and turn right up a footpath. To the left is the barn belonging to Copdock Hall. At the path junction turn right and cross the stile. Cross the next stile and follow the fence line to another stile, then descend, and at the bottom, turn left. The path swings right past the old mill, crosses the mill stream, then veers left. At the footpath junction bear right, back up to the end of the dual carriageway. Cross and follow the pavement into Washbrook. At the road junction go left along 'The Street'. The Brook Inn is on the right.

PLACES OF INTEREST NEARBY

Christchurch Mansion in Ipswich is set in attractive parkland. Free to enter, it is a Tudor mansion with period furnished rooms and an art gallery including works by Constable.

9 **Cotton**
3.5 miles (5.5 km)

WALK HIGHLIGHTS
The ancient scattered village of Cotton is noted for its many moated farms and old buildings, one of which, Hempnalls Hall, you pass on the walk. Cotton was reputedly used as a meeting place by the conspirators in the Gunpowder Plot. A Suffolk man, Ambrose Rookwood who was one of the main conspirators, was executed on Tower Hill. Look out for Carter's Meadow which has beehives and over 40 species of wild flower.

THE PUB
The Trowel & Hammer www.trowelandhammercotton.com
☎ 01449 781234 **IP14 4QL**

THE WALK
Turn left out of the pub and immediately, behind the hedge of the last house on the right, there is a footpath into a small meadow. This leads to a larger field and you go down to a little wood and across a bridge.

Guide to Suffolk Pub Walks

HOW TO GET THERE: From the B1113 Stanton Road that runs between Finningham & Stowmarket, turn into Blacksmith Road just north of Bacton. Then right into Mill Road and the pub is on the right. **Postcode** IP14 4QL

MAP: OS Explorer 211 Bury St Edmunds & Stowmarket.

PARKING: The pub is happy for walkers to park in the overflow car park adjoining the pub.

When you reach the footpath crossroads soon after, go left alongside the large crop field with a hedge on the left. Go for some distance almost to the end of the field. Just before the corner, go left through a wooden gate and trees to a wooden bridge by the road.

2 Turn right and keep to the road as it swings right. At the road junction go straight on to Dandy Corner. The road veers sharply right.

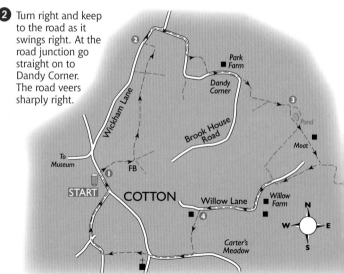

A little further along go left through an opening in the hedge onto a field edge footpath, which swings right following the hedge and goes back to the lane. Turn left along the lane passing Park Farm, then, just as the road bends right, take the footpath on the left, going around the metal gate and alongside a high hedge. The path bends sharp right then, in the corner of the field, swings left along the field edge. Continue on and just before the path bends right again, look out for a footpath through the trees on the right.

Pass a pond on the left and after an outbuilding on the right, go straight on at the next path marker post. You then come to the moat of Hempnalls Hall. At the end, by the brick gateway, turn right then straight away left. At the next footpath post soon after, turn right along a wide grass path between the deep ditch and the field. This eventually emerges onto the access road where you continue in the same direction to a little junction by Willow Farm. Turn right and continue along the lane (Willow Lane) for some distance until you see a footpath sign on the left by Mallard Hall.

Pass the wooden bridge on the right and go straight on, passing crop fields until you reach the field corner where you bear right to the road. Turn right past houses going uphill to the church. Go through the metal gates leading into the churchyard and take the path around to the other side of the church, where you exit via a grass path. Continue to where you cross a stile into a field, then through a wooden gate and over another stile to the road. Turn right to the crossroads where you go straight over (to Finningham) and proceed to the end of this narrow lane. At the T-junction, turn left and the pub is a little way down on the left.

PLACES OF INTEREST NEARBY

Cotton, although only a tiny village, has its own unusual **Mechanical Music Museum** which is open every Sunday afternoon. It can also be booked for private tours. It has a 1926 Wurlitzer organ, which lived in the Leicester Square Theatre for over 30 years until the 1960s, and a playing demonstration takes place every Sunday. There is free parking, toilets, refreshments and a souvenirs kiosk.
www.mechanicalmusicmuseum.co.uk

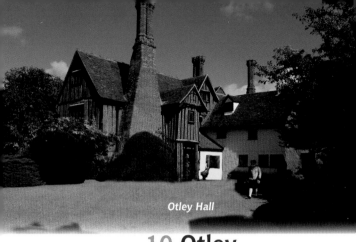

Otley Hall

10 Otley
4 miles (6.4 km)

WALK HIGHLIGHTS
This is a pleasant walk around the rolling fields of the small village of
Otley. Children and dogs are welcome at the pub and you can pre-order
food, to be ready when you return from your walk. There is plenty to see
en route including Otley Hall, a Grade I listed moated hall dating from
1512. It was once the home of Bartholomew Gosnold, who led the first
recorded European expedition to Cape Cod. Today, it is still a private
home but the gardens and café are open on a Wednesday from May to
September. www.otleyhall.co.uk

THE PUB
The White Hart www.thewhitehartotley.co.uk
☎ 01473 890312 **IP6 9NS**

THE WALK
1 From the pub car park, turn left along the road (watch out for traffic)
and soon after turn right along the byway which is the tarmac access
road to Grange Farm. After you pass the pond on the right the surface

32

HOW TO GET THERE: Otley lies on the B1079 between Woodbridge and Helmingham. The pub is on this main road just north of the village. **Postcode** IP6 9NS

MAP: OS Explorer 211 Bury St Edmunds & Stowmarket.

PARKING: Use the pub car park but check with the landlord first.

converts to grass. Continue along this wide path bordered by hedges. At the crossroads continue straight on. At the next fork you can go either way but taking the option to the right gives you glimpses of Otley Hall through the trees on the right. Continue to the road.

Turn right along the road. On the right is Otley Hall, although unfortunately its magnificent façade is not really visible from the road. Further along, take the footpath on the left, by the edge of the field. Cross a wooden bridge and continue along a narrow but

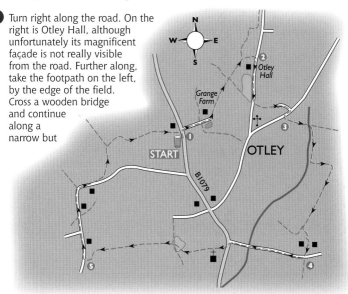

well trodden path between hedges. Cross another bridge and turn left into a residential cul de sac. This bends right to the main road.

3 Turn right and a little further along on the left take the bridleway which soon stretches out into open farmland. After the ditch turn right, following the line of the ditch. Otley church can be seen in the distance. At the corner of the field turn left and follow the hedge line, going gently uphill. You are then forced right, over the ditch. After some distance you pass through a wooden gate in the hedge on your left. Head for the barn at the centre of the other side of the meadow and pass the wooden barns. The track takes you to the lane.

4 Turn right and proceed along the lane all the way to the end. At the main road, turn left and almost immediately, take the next footpath on the right, leading to the church. Go around the church to the right and exit by the back of the churchyard. Cross a ditch and follow the path with the hedge on your left. Cross some planks then go through a tiny wood. Cross over a bridge and bear right, following the field edge as it bends left. Keep the hedge to your right, going gently uphill. At the end the path passes a cottage and reaches a lane.

5 Turn right along the lane. Pass some pretty cottages. The road bends sharp right and after Ashfield Cottage, look out for a footpath on the left with a wooden stile next to a metal gate. This takes you onto a wide grass path which bends left around the edge of the field. Soon after passing into the next field, turn right at the footpath junction, keeping to the right of the hedge. Stay on the grass strip which bends one way and then the other, then over the stream and bears left to take you back to the road. Turn right for the White Hart pub.

PLACES OF INTEREST NEARBY

Helmingham Hall lies just two miles north of Otley. It is privately owned, being in the Tollemache family for 18 generations. The gardens, open to the public from May to September, consist of 400 acres and contain both red and fallow deer. John Constable painted at this spot.
www.helmingham.com

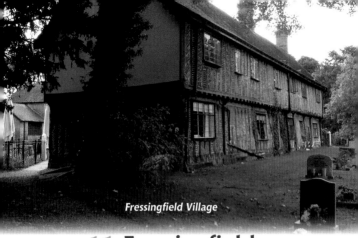

Fressingfield Village

11 Fressingfield
3.2 miles (5.2 km)

WALK HIGHLIGHTS
Fressingfield has a reputation for being one of the prettiest villages in Suffolk. I decided to keep this walk quite short so there is time to admire all it has to offer. Where you exit the church at the end of the walk, there is an information board to the right by the pond. This is called the Village Heritage map and has all the listed buildings in Fressingfield, no fewer than 57 of them! Even the pub dates from 1508 when it was a guildhall. It was later used as the village poor house, before becoming a pub in 1710.

THE PUB
The Fox and Goose www.foxandgoose.net
☎ 01379 586247 **IP21 5PB**

THE WALK
From the pub, turn right along the road past the chapel with the ornate chimney. Just before the next road junction take the short walkway on the right and at the road, turn right past Woodyard Cottage and then the

Guide to Suffolk Pub Walks

HOW TO GET THERE: Fressingfield lies on the B1116 between Harleston and Dennington. The Fox and Goose is next to the church in Church Street. **Postcode** IP21 5PB

MAP: OS Explorer 230 Diss & Harleston.

PARKING: Walkers can park in the pub car park but please let the proprietor know first.

little village shop. Continue along the road through the village and past the Methodist chapel. Turn right just the other side of the hedge at Post Mill Lane along a grass path. After a pond you are in open farmland. Go gently down alongside a brook to where you cross a track and follow the footpath sign straight on.

2 Descend again to a wooden bridge where the undulating path narrows. There are good views of the rolling countryside to the left. Cross through the hedge line. Here the path goes across the

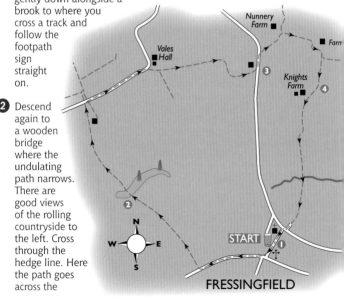

field but the farmer stated that most walkers go left around the field to the red brick farm building and turn left along the track to the lane. Turn right along this pretty lane. When you reach the corner by Vales Hall, turn right onto a footpath which follows the main track past the farm buildings. Keep to the right of the high hedge along a wide track, which later curves sharply right between the fields then back left to the thatched house by the road.

3 Turn left along the main road keeping to the verge on the right-hand side. Soon you turn right at Nunnery Farm along a footpath following the concrete access road. At the farm just past the pink cottage, turn right onto an unsigned straight footpath. Just before the house at the end go right then left over the ditch following the hedge line. Then go right along the stony track but as this bends left, you go straight on, along a grass path between the ditch and the field, then across the field to the right of the wind turbine.

4 Continue across a culvert and into the next field by Knights Farm where you have a distant view of Fressingfield church. Continue along the edge of the field. The path goes right and then left the other side of the ditch. At the next corner go straight on across the crop field to the wide gap in the trees. Cross the stream and go back uphill. At the track junction go straight on but to the left of the ditch, then down into the village by the bridge and the road. Turn right and at the corner of the next road junction go through the white gate into the churchyard to admire the red brick and timber façade of the back of the Fox and Goose pub. Exit by the main gate and turn right for the pub.

PLACES OF INTEREST NEARBY

Wingfield Barns, in the village next door, has an art gallery, coffee shop, gift shop, beautiful gardens and a programme of art exhibitions, theatre productions and concerts. www.wingfieldbarns.com IP21 5RA

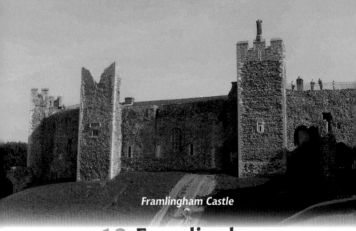

Framlingham Castle

12 Framlingham
4.5 miles (7.1 km)

WALK HIGHLIGHTS
This walk takes in part of the town, follows the River Ore and reveals some lovely open countryside. Its historic buildings, the castle, St Michael's church, the Victorian Framlingham College and the water tower are constant landmarks that can be viewed on the way.

THE PUB
The Crown www.theframlinghamcrown.co.uk
☎ 01728 723521 **IP13 9AP**

THE WALK
1 From the pub in Market Square turn right up Market Hill. When you reach Church Street take the footpath on the left which runs alongside the Castle Inn and the castle moat (on the right if you have parked in the Castle car park). Bear left and descend to a wooden gate. Ahead is a large lake called the Mere and behind it is Framlingham College. Turn right. The path swings right then left through a gate. Keep left along a well trodden path. Continue on to the footbridge

HOW TO GET THERE: Framlingham lies at the junction of the B1116 and B1119 and the Crown pub is in Market Square. **Postcode** IP13 9BP

MAP: OS Explorer 212 Woodbridge & Saxmundham.

PARKING: Park in the pay and display car park at the castle, next to Castle Inn.

and bear right. Follow the stream around the playing field, crossing a bridge at the other end, to the lane.

2 Turn left and soon after the road bends left, take the footpath on the right through another kissing gate. Look for a concealed sign soon after and turn right to follow the hedge line uphill with the hedge on your right. At the top, turn right again by the farm, between the hedge and the fence. Cross a bridge over the brook where you are guided left by the footpath arrows, then

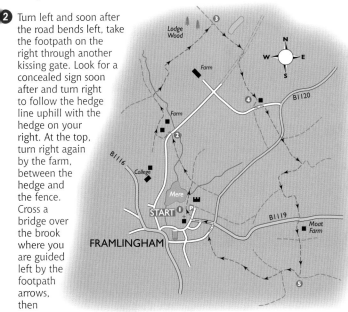

right, then immediately left again across the field. At the end of the field by the stream, cross a stile and go right over the wooden bridge and uphill along the edge of the field. Swing left at the far corner, then right following the telegraph wires. Follow this all the way to the end, passing a wood on your left. At the footpath T-junction turn right.

3 Continue to the end along a wide track and when you reach a little lane, turn right. Soon after, look out for a footpath on the left going at an angle across the crop field. At the other side, by the gap in the hedge, go straight across the next field, heading towards the white cottage. Bear right alongside the cottage to the lane. Turn left and take the next footpath on the right along a narrow path. You emerge into a field. Proceed to the gate in the hedge on the other side by the road.

4 Take the footpath opposite going gently uphill. The castle and church can be seen to the right. At the end you cross a ditch to a path T-junction. Turn right and follow the field edge, the path follows the line of the ditch around the field. At the next path junction go straight on towards the water tower along a path which bends a number of times to the road by Moat Farm. Follow the path on the other side that immediately runs to the right of the hedge and goes around the field edge. When you reach the footpath crossroads at the end of the field, go straight on along a wide grass path for some distance to the next junction (Cold Hall Lane).

5 Turn right along an even wider grass track between hedges. Where the path forks, keep left along a grass path between fields. This meanders for some distance to join a stony track, which bends right and leads up to the road. Turn right along the pavement and then left at the next road junction along Castle Street. Continue on past the cottages and turn left at the bottom, passing the church again and returning into Market Square.

PLACES OF INTEREST NEARBY

Framlingham Castle is a 12th-century fortress which is now owned by English Heritage. It was previously owned by the Dukes of Norfolk, although it was frequently forfeited to the crown. It was the home of Mary Tudor in 1553 when she became queen.
www.englishheritage.org.uk

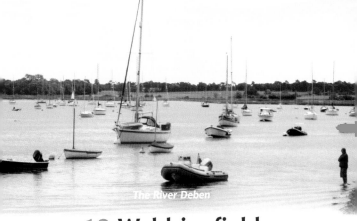

The River Deben

13 Waldringfield

4 miles (6.4 km)

WALK HIGHLIGHTS

Towards the end of the 19th century, Mason's cement-making industry sprang up in Waldringfield, using mud from the river. Served by 100 barges a month, the industry survived until 1907. This walk takes you by the River Deben and through some lovely Suffolk countryside. There are river cruises available nearby but you have to pre-book.
www.waldringfieldboatyard.co.uk

THE PUB

The Maybush www.debeninns.co.uk
☎ 01473 736215 **IP12 4QL**

THE WALK

From the car park, return to the road and turn right leading down to the river. Turn right at the river again by the front of the Maybush pub and continue along the beach. As you pass the sailing club, use the raised path, and go through the boatyard where, after the last chalet, you are forced right. Ignore the footpath on the left but continue straight on to the end of the boatyard, through a little wood and over a wooden

Guide to Suffolk Pub Walks

HOW TO GET THERE: From the A12 south of Woodbridge, at the Brightwell roundabout take the Heath Road exit signed to Waldringfield. Follow the signs to the village for about 2 miles. Go right through the village to the river where the pub and car park are on the right. **Postcode** IP12 4QL

MAP: OS Explorer 197 Ipswich, Felixstowe & Harwich.

PARKING: There is a public car park next to the pub and you can claim back your pay and display money if you are using the pub.

footbridge. Pass a lake on the left. The path swings left around the lake and goes gently up through successive crop fields, with good views of the river to your left. Pass a house and go right up a track. This takes you to Plum Tree Cottage by the lane.

2 Go sharp left just before the lane on a bridleway, around a metal gate and along a concrete track. This later becomes a tree-lined dirt track with good views of the River Deben to the left. Proceed for some distance. At Hemley Hall bear slightly left before the gate. As you pass the cottages the path becomes a lane. At the end of the lane is a road T-junction by the handsome red brick Tudor tower of Hemley church (usually open).

3 Turn right up the road. Pass Church Farm and soon after leave the road taking the footpath on the left. A good wide path takes you through farmland and fields of poppies in the summer. The path then veers right and descends to a metal gate. Go through a field and another gate then into a field of lovely silvery ash trees. On the other side of a brook, turn right and continue along a boardwalk then pass a children's play area to the road.

4 Turn right along the road past Newbourne Hall. At the road junction follow the sign to Waldringfield taking you to the Fox Inn, where you may wish to take a rest. Otherwise continue along the road, going straight on at the next road junction. Soon after, just as the road curves right, take the footpath on the left. The path winds through a thicket then fairly steeply up steps to a wide path, and through a field, taking you to a lane.

WALDRINGFIELD

The Maybush

START

FB

Lake

River Deben

The Fox Inn

Newbourne

Hemley Hall

Hemley

Turn left and follow the lane for a short distance. At the first bend where the road goes sharp right, take the wide footpath on the left. Pass between fields and continue straight on through a crop field then an area of trees and shrub. At the footpath junction turn right by a corn field and emerge at the lane. Take the footpath opposite into a meadow (where there is a seat for resting and admiring the view of the river) and then through a field to the road. Now turn right down the road which takes you back to the Maybush.

PLACES OF INTEREST NEARBY

Sutton Hoo, near Woodbridge, is where the Saxon King Raedwald was buried in his ship. The excavation of 1939 revealed a magnificent collection of artefacts, including the famous Saxon bronze helmet. www.nationaltrust.org.uk/suttonhoo

14 Yoxford

4 miles (6.4 km)

WALK HIGHLIGHTS
Within a few minutes' walk from the centre of Yoxford you are out into the countryside. This simple route to the north of the village passes through farmland and a pleasant open landscape. The village derives its name from a ford of the River Yox, where oxen could pass. Every year, on the Sunday after Easter, the village holds a brawn eating competition (known locally as Pork Cheese). During the event a Brawn Queen is picked from the village and her first job as Queen is to ceremoniously cut the cheese.

THE PUB
The Griffin (no website but lots of reviews on tripadvisor)
☎ 01728 668229 **IP17 3EP**

THE WALK
1 From the pub, turn right along the High Street to St Andrew's church where you cross the road and, just the other side of the little shop, by

HOW TO GET THERE: Yoxford lies on the junction where the A12 connects to the A1120. The Griffin is in the High Street almost next to the church. **Postcode** IP17 3EP

MAP: OS Explorer 231 Southwold and Bungay.

PARKING: The landowner is quite happy for you to use the pub car park, but check first as a courtesy.

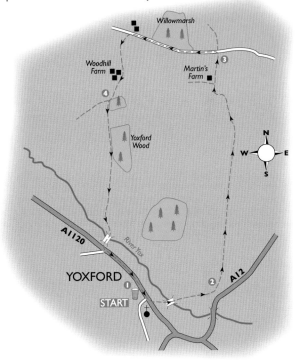

the attractive red brick building, take the footpath through the gate and alongside the wicker fence. Proceed through a wooded area and over the River Yox, then gently uphill on a grass path between fences. At the end cross over a track and go onto a long, straight, grass footpath between fences.

2 Proceed up to a wooden footbridge and continue through the middle of a large field. At the end, go through a gap in the hedge into the next field and then through a new tree plantation. At the end, bear right through a gap in the hedge and swing left on the other side onto a footpath through the field. The path turns slightly left with the hedge to your right. Go uphill to the field corner where you are forced left, then turn right soon after by the lonesome tree. At Martin's Farm continue straight on up a wide concrete track which takes you to the lane.

3 Turn left along the lane. Pass Willowmarsh Wood on the right. When you reach North Boundary Farm, take the footpath opposite on the left, following the telegraph poles. At the end of the field, follow the way-markers turning left, then immediately right. As the track bends right, go straight on through the metal gateway and follow the wooden fence to your right. As the fence turns 90 degrees right, go straight on and head for the metal gate in the far corner of the field.

4 On the other side is a footpath junction. Bear left, going alongside the trees and after a gap, follow a wide grass path with a hedge to the left. At the end of Yoxford Wood, continue straight on then descend gently for some distance until you reach the footbridge, where you turn right, back over the River Yox on a wide track to the main road. Turn left along the pavement back into the village High Street and your starting place.

PLACES OF INTEREST NEARBY

Just half a mile west of the village is the **Yoxford Antiques Centre**, open every day except Tuesday. There is a wide mixture of antiques and collectables for both interior and outside from over 70 dealers. Staff are on hand to give information and advice. There is ample free parking, a café for drinks and light snacks and toilet facilities.
www.yoxfordantiques.com IP17 3JW

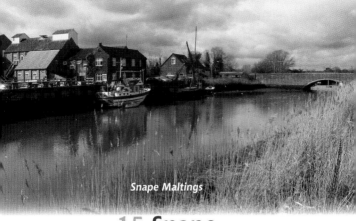

Snape Maltings

15 Snape
3.8 miles (6 km)

WALK HIGHLIGHTS
This village walk includes a section of the Sailors' Path by the serene River Alde, and then out into the surrounding countryside to the area known as Gromford. The Snape wetland is managed by the Suffolk Wildlife Trust and is in a designated Area of Outstanding Natural Beauty. The mudflats are a haven for many wading birds, such as the curlew and oyster catcher. Look out for otter colonies, barn owls and rare plants such as the yellow marsh sow-thistle and the pink southern marsh orchid. The 15th-century smugglers pub welcomes children and dogs and the menu is mostly made up from locally grown produce and home-reared meat.

THE PUB
The Crown Inn www.snape-crown.co.uk
☎ 01728 688324 **IP17 1SL**

THE WALK
Turn left out of the pub car park, and follow the pavement on the other side of the road. Cross back over when you reach the road bridge and take the footpath on the left, which follows the north side of the river

Guide to Suffolk Pub Walks

HOW TO GET THERE: From the A1094 between the A12 south of Saxmundham and Aldeburgh, turn south onto the B1069 taking you to Snape village. The pub is at the south end of the village by the crossroads. **Postcode** IP17 1SL

MAP: OS Explorer 212 Woodbridge & Saxmundham.

PARKING: You are welcome to use the large pub car park, but check with the landlord as a courtesy.

bank. This is called the Sailors' Path. On the opposite side of the river is the famous Snape Maltings. Continue along a sandy, raised path which meanders alongside the river. In the distance can be seen the tower of Iken church. Along the way are two information boards telling you about the wildlife that can be seen on the Snape marshes and mudflats. After some distance, when you eventually reach the path T-junction by the log seat in the trees, turn left through the woods.

2 Continue to follow the Sailors' Path. At the footpath junction go straight on and the same again at the next one. Proceed gently uphill and straight on to the lane. Go straight ahead along the lane, passing the White House and Rookery Farm. At the top of the lane, just as it bends to the right, turn left along a wide footpath towards the distant church. Continue through a mixed landscape of farm fields, gorse and heathland to the road.

3 At the road take the footpath opposite onto a wide stony path which curves right to a road junction. Here you immediately turn left down Wadd Lane, running behind the petrol station. Look out for the footpath further along on the left by the passing place. Keep left alongside the fence, then downhill between crop fields to the thatched cottage by the road junction.

4 Take the 'No through lane' opposite. Pass some cottages and at the end of the lane, the path narrows, continuing along a grass surface. The path turns sharp left. Go gently uphill to the lane and turn right, travelling along the lane which leads back to Snape village. Pass the Methodist

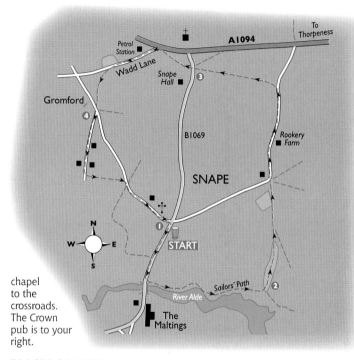

chapel
to the
crossroads.
The Crown
pub is to your
right.

PLACES OF INTEREST NEARBY

At **Snape Maltings** are a collection of interesting shops, galleries and curiosities in the converted old mill buildings. There are art galleries featuring a selection of British artists, antique shops, boutiques, and other shops, plus cafés and tearooms. It is all set in a lovely location on the south side of the River Alde.

If you enjoy art then a few miles east is the coastal resort of **Aldeburgh** where there are many little galleries and art shops.

Orford Castle

16 Orford
3.2 miles (5.3 km)

WALK HIGHLIGHTS
Orford Castle is a dominant feature in the town and the magnificent keep is a major landmark on the walk. There is also the River Ore with its boats and watercraft and a distant lighthouse to admire, not to mention some lovely countryside. The pub is one of the oldest in Suffolk, dating from the 13th century and children and dogs are welcome. The town has a reputation for good food and is famous for its oysters.

THE PUB
The Kings Head Inn www.thekingsheadorford.co.uk
☎ 01394 450271 **IP12 2LW**

THE WALK
1 From the pub car park walk past the pub and turn right into Market Hill (the market square) heading towards the castle. Just before the Crown and Castle hotel, turn left down Crown Lane which is a narrow pedestrian walkway. Go all the way to the bottom and turn left, passing

HOW TO GET THERE: From the A12 north of Ipswich if approaching from the south take the A1152 at Woodbridge and then the B1084 or the B1078 from the north. Head for the town centre. The pub is on the B1084 next to the church. **Postcode** IP12 2LW

MAP: OS Explorer 212 Woodbridge & Saxmundham.

PARKING: The Kings Head car park in Front Street is located on the other side of the craft shop next to the pub, but check with the landlord first. There is also free parking in Market Hill. IP12 2NZ.

some old cottages. At the main street turn right and pass the Jolly Sailor pub to where the road ends at the quay.

Turn right behind the last building by Quay House on a concrete path by the edge of the River Ore. The route then continues on a

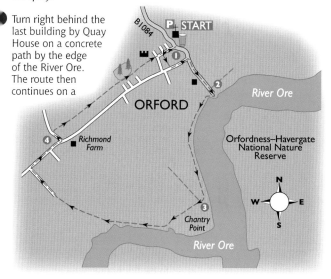

raised grass path with wonderful views of the river boats to the left and on the right the Castle and the church in the distance. You pass over a pillbox where the path narrows. There is an alternative parallel path to the right at the bottom of the bank if you need shelter from the wind but you lose the river views. Continue to the wooden gate.

3 Here you turn right down the bank and cross the bridge. Continue along a good grass path to another bridge, and back up to the bank on the sea wall. Bear right along the sea wall and continue for some distance, enjoying the panorama of the Suffolk landscape. Just after the path swings left, continue down the bank to the right and through a metal gate. Follow a long straight path between fields. It converts to a gravel track between hedges, taking you to the lane. Turn right along this quiet road. The castle can be seen ahead. After a long straight stretch of about a quarter of a mile, where the road kinks, turn left onto a wide sandy footpath.

4 Soon after look out for steps on the right. Take this footpath and as the track curves right, go straight on heading directly towards the castle (the path may not be very well defined). At the other end there is a small gap in the hedge and on the other side you follow a wide grass path between crops. At the end of this field go straight on through the hedge, cross a track and continue on a straight path towards Orford Castle. At the bungalow cross another track and, slightly to the right, take the path through the trees. You suddenly emerge at the castle. Continue through the car park and at the road turn left and uphill back to Market Hill and the Kings Head.

PLACES OF INTEREST NEARBY

Orford Castle is owned by English Heritage. It was built during the reign of Henry II in the 12th century. It remained the property of the Kings of England until 1336 when it was sold to the Earl of Suffolk. It was opened to the public in 1930 and houses a museum. Open from April to November. www.english-heritage.org.uk

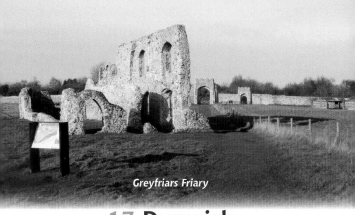

Greyfriars Friary

17 Dunwich

3.1 miles (5 km)

WALK HIGHLIGHTS

Dunwich was once a thriving port, one of the largest in England, but due to coastal erosion, most of the village now lies underneath the sea. It is said you can still hear the church bells underneath the waves. The little Dunwich Museum, which you pass at the end of the walk, is fascinating and well worth a visit as it provides an understanding of what happened to the village over the centuries. The dog-friendly pub is the only one in the village and is over 400 years old. Supposedly it was once the haunt of smugglers.

THE PUB

The Ship www.shipatdunwich.co.uk
☎ 01728 648219 **IP17 3DT**

THE WALK

Go to the little road junction next to the pub where you will see the footpath which takes you up steps and through trees. At the fork keep left and continue up to the cliff edge. To the left is the sea and on your right are the ruins of the old Franciscan friary. Continue past the last grave

Guide to Suffolk Pub Walks

HOW TO GET THERE: Dunwich can be reached from the A12. Just north of Yoxford take the road signed to Westleton village. Go through the village and onto the Dunwich Road. At the fork as you approach the village, bear right to the pub. **Postcode** IP17 3DT

MAP: OS Explorer 231 Southwold & Bungay.

PARKING: There are usually spaces along the road opposite the pub (St James Street).

of All Saints church and then the friary entrance with an information board. Continue on to a path junction where you turn right between the friary wall and a fence. Then turn left through a gap in the wall into the wood. At the end of the wood is a footpath junction with a way-marker post.

2 Turn right along a wide stony path, past cottages and houses. Pass through a wooden gate onto the road and continue along the road for a short distance before taking the next footpath on the left (to the Dairy House), along a tarmac track. Pass through a mature woodland, past a house and onto a track. Go through a gate, then stay on the main track through the trees. Cross a track and continue on until you eventually emerge at the lane.

3 Take the bridleway almost opposite, along a wide path between bushes and scrub, going very gently uphill. When you reach the path crossroads at the top, at the corner of the heath, turn right. Pass Mount Pleasant Farm and proceed straight on along a wide track. When you get to the road, go straight over going downhill along a good track. At the end by the farm, you reach another path junction.

4 Turn right and follow the shady footpath through trees for some distance. At the end turn right onto the lane, following the signs to the museum and the beach. Pass the church on your right and continue along the lane past cottages and the museum then back to the Ship Inn.

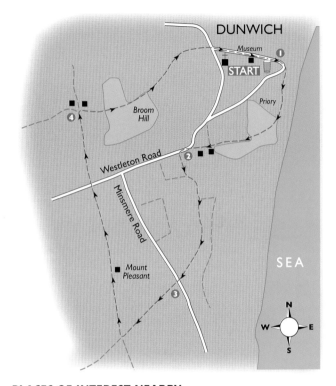

PLACES OF INTEREST NEARBY

Immediately to the south of Dunwich is the RSPB's **Minsmere Nature Reserve**, popular with wildlife lovers. It has become very well known, being the host for the BBC programmes *Springwatch* and *Autumnwatch*. It is not only excellent for birds such as avocets and bitterns, but within the reserve are otters, lizards and water voles. There is also a café, bookshop and a children's play area.

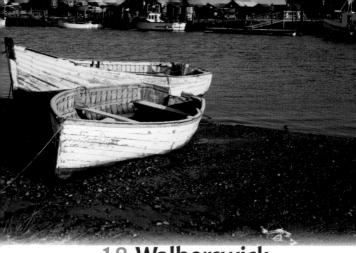

18 Walberswick

4.3 miles (7 km)

WALK HIGHLIGHTS

Walberswick is a charming Suffolk village by the sea with tea shops, pubs and a beach of sand dunes. This walk, which circumnavigates the village, takes in sea views, woods, Walberswick Common and the riverside walk by the River Blyth, using coastal paths and well known trails.

THE PUB

The Bell bellinnwalberswick.co.uk
☎ 01502 723109 **IP18 6TN**

THE WALK

1 From the pub head down towards the harbour. At the public car park turn right into the car park, (there is a footpath sign on the corner) and on the other side, just before the bridge, go right again alongside the creek. Go up the steps at the end and along an unmade road. Just before the thatched shelter, turn left along the footpath onto a wide stony path. At the fork, bear right onto a track that runs parallel with the shoreline.

HOW TO GET THERE: Turn off the A12 just south of Blythburgh onto the B1387 which takes you directly into the village. **Postcode** IP18 6TA

MAP: OS Explorer 231 Southwold & Bungay.

PARKING: There is a paying car park at the end of the road by the harbour.

At the end turn right up a bank onto a narrow path that winds through the trees and undergrowth. At the path junction turn left and go straight on between a hedge and a fence. When you reach the next junction by the old ruin, turn left along the bridleway.

2 Proceed straight on by the reed beds. The path bends right and goes uphill to a seat with fine sea views and past a concrete bunker. When you reach the next path junction, turn left soon continuing through trees. It bends one way and then the other, passing another seat and then onto a long boardwalk between the reed marshes. Where it ends, turn right, then at the path

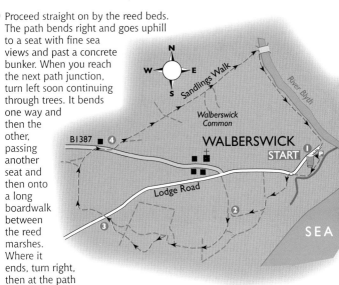

crossroads soon after go right again. Pass through a wooded area to the lane.

3 Cross the road and take the bridleway opposite. The path bends right at the trees and goes gently uphill. Where the fence ends turn right onto a grass path (Sandlings Walk), through a gate and across a field to the road by the red brick cottage. Turn right along the road (watch out for fast moving traffic) for a short distance then cross over and take the bridleway on the left.

4 The route runs across Walberswick Common. Cross a track and go straight on. When you reach a path junction proceed through the wooden gate and continue straight on, still following Sandlings Walk. Ahead in the distance is the Southwold lighthouse. Continue for some distance until you reach a little lane. Turn left along the lane. This is a bridleway. Follow this all the way to the river. Before the bridge turn right along the sea wall. Continue all the way along this raised path by the river to the wooden sheds at Walberswick Harbour, where you turn right back to the car park and the pub.

PLACES OF INTEREST NEARBY

Just the other side of the River Blyth is the seaside resort of **Southwold**, probably the most popular seaside resort in Suffolk. It has beaches and beach huts, a pier and a magnificent white lighthouse (the town's trademark). You can tour the **Adnams Brewery** which supplies most of the pubs featured in this book. Southwold is an old-fashioned town which is what gives it its charm. There are quaint shops and tearooms along the main street and a very unusual amber shop and museum, which is the largest and oldest of its kind in the UK. You can take the ferry from Walberswick Harbour to Southwold, or walk via the Bailey Bridge which you pass on your walk.

19 Blyford

4.5 miles or 5.5 miles (7.2km or 8.8km)

WALK HIGHLIGHTS
This pretty walk takes you through meadows and across bridges by the banks of the River Blyth, which divides Blyford from Wenhaston.

THE PUB
The Queen's Head www.queensheadblyford.co.uk
☎ 01502 478404 **IP19 9JY**

THE WALK
From the pub car park, cross the main road and take the lane opposite leading to Wenhaston. At the road bridge over the river, take the footpath over the stile on the right and follow the riverside path. Pass a rickety bridge into the next field and then a stile. After a while you cross a river tributary by a footbridge. Keep to the left, heading for the stile in the corner of the meadow and a wooden bridge. The path runs close to the river bank. Then go over another wooden bridge and on a path through a semi-wooded area. Cross a stile into a large meadow. Then

59

Guide to Suffolk Pub Walks

HOW TO GET THERE: Blyford lies on the B1123 between Southwold and Halesworth. The pub is on the main road opposite the church at the Wenhaston turn off. **Postcode** IP19 9JY

MAP: OS Explorer 231 Southwold and Bungay.

PARKING: The pub has a very spacious car park which you can use whilst on your walk, but check with the landlord first.

over successive stiles by the old ash tree. Follow the river bank and over one more stile to the lane.

2 Turn left over the road bridge and keep left at the fork in the road, passing the ruins of a chapel. At the T-junction, almost opposite and just to the left, follow a footpath by the golf course. Keep close to the hedgerow on your right all the way to the 7th tee. Turn left at the wooden gate (do not go through it) and go to the corner of the field where you go right, across a bridge.

3 Walk diagonally across the field (if there are crops follow the field edge).

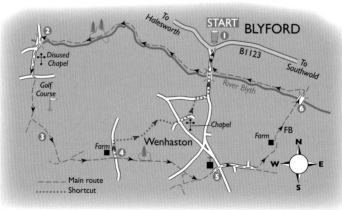

On the far side is a footpath post leading you to a T-junction. Go left into the next field, and at the end of this field, by an oak tree, look out for a way-marker post pointing diagonally right across a little meadow. At the far corner, cross a stile by the pond into the next meadow. Cross a ditch then left by a large field with the hedgerow on your left to the lane. For the shorter route of 4½ miles see the instructions below. Otherwise:

4 Take the footpath directly opposite. Continue for some distance keeping the hedge on your left. Pass a little wood on your left and continue straight on to the cottage by the lane. Once again take the footpath almost opposite running by the horse paddocks. The path curves left by the playing field and converts to a lane with a hard surface, passing some cottages and the parish church of St Peter of Wenhaston.

5 Go straight over by the village hall along Narrow Way, passing cottages and houses. After Blowes Piece, where Narrow Way ends, take the path on the left by a wide track which leads to farm land. At the farm follow the track to a gate where you bear slightly left and look out for a very narrow gap through the hedge on the left. Continue between the electric fence on the left and the hedge on the right to a footbridge, then another bridge with metal gates at either end.

6 Cross the bridge then turn left to follow the river bank. Continue for some distance, passing through a metal kissing gate until you reach the road bridge kissing gate, where you turn right and walk back to the pub.

SHORTCUT

Turn left up the lane, passing Bartholomew's Farm. Take the next footpath on the right. Continue to a farm access track to the road. Take Chapel Lane opposite. Pass the little chapel and where the road bends right, go straight on along a footpath. Keep going straight, descending to the lane. Turn right along the lane and at the road T-junction turn left, back to the bridge and straight on to return to the pub.

PLACES OF INTEREST NEARBY

Just two miles west of Blyford is the market town of **Halesworth**, which still has its market in the square every Wednesday. The old almshouses are now an art gallery.

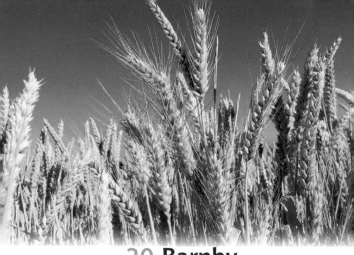

20 Barnby
3 miles (4.8 km)

WALK HIGHLIGHTS
During the walk you pass a garden centre, the Swan pub and the 13th-century church of St John the Baptist. The church is unusual in that it has a thatched roof. It also contains magnificent stained glass windows and some restored wall paintings. This walk will take you towards the rural village of Mutford, through farmland, large fields and quiet lanes.

THE PUB
The Swan Inn (no website but lots of good reviews on tripadvisor)
☎ 01502 476646 **NR34 7QF**

THE WALK
1 From the front of the pub, take the narrow road leading east away from the pub which is Swan Lane. Go to the end of the lane and take care in crossing the busy main road. Take the footpath opposite, leading to the church of St John the Baptist. When you go through the iron gates bear left around the church and follow the narrow footpath by a fence.

HOW TO GET THERE: Barnby lies on the A146 between Beccles and Lowestoft. About 2 miles east of Beccles, take a left turn into Barnby and take the first turning right into Swan Lane. The pub is about a quarter of a mile along on the left. **Postcode** NR34 7QF

MAP: OS Explorer OL40 The Broads.

PARKING: Only use the pub car park if you will be visiting the pub afterwards and please inform the landlord. Otherwise, you can park on the roads around the pub.

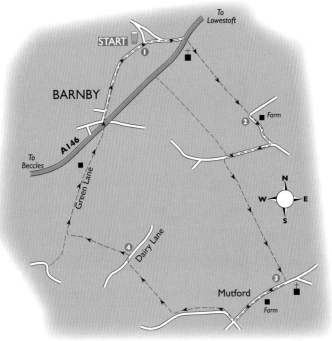

Continue over a ditch and through a wooded area. Cross a planked bridge into a crop field. Bear right along the field edge, taking you to the lane.

2 Go straight on along the lane, passing Pond Farm, to the T-junction by the pond. Turn right towards Beccles and proceed along the straight road. After passing a footpath on the right, take the next footpath soon after on the left. This is a narrow path running straight through the field. Head towards the church tower in the distance. The path widens and follows a hedge to your left. At the road is St Andrew's church, Mutford, with its unusual tower. Turn right along the road.

3 Pass Manor Farm and at the crossroads by the telephone box, turn right, signed to North Cove. Just before the speed limit signs, look out for a raised permissive path through a gap on the right, which runs parallel to the lane. At the end turn right along the footpath going gently uphill with distant countryside views to the left. This is a long straight path by a field which ends at Dairy Lane.

4 Turn right at the lane then immediately left onto the footpath. This is a good field edge path in open countryside. At the next path junction just past the perished oak tree, turn right along the byway. Pass a house to the left and continue towards the road. Before the end go left through the gap to cross back over the busy main road. After the Barnby sign, turn right along Swan Lane, passing the nursery. The pavement runs out but not too far further along on the left is the Swan pub.

PLACES OF INTEREST NEARBY

Lowestoft is a few miles to the east of Barnby and is a traditional seaside resort with a beach and two piers. **Pleasurewood Hills** is a theme park on the north side of the town. There is a harbour with fishing boats and Oulton Broad to the west is the most southerly point of the Broads, with boat trips or boats for hire.

Beccles, to the west, is a much quieter town where you can relax by the River Waveney. There is a small museum and a fortnightly farmers' market.